# THE BEST YEARS?

# THE BEST YEARS?

## Reflections of School Leavers
## in the 1980s

edited by Joan Hughes

ABERDEEN UNIVERSITY PRESS

First published 1984
Aberdeen University Press
A member of the Pergamon Group
© Centre for Educational Sociology
University of Edinburgh 1984

**British Library Cataloguing in Publication Data**
The Best years?
   1.   High school students – Scotland
   2.   High school graduates – Employment – Scotland
   3.   Unemployment – Scotland
I. Hughes, J.M.
373.18′092′2     LA656.7

ISBN 0-08-030405-2

PRINTED IN GREAT BRITAIN
THE UNIVERSITY OF EDINBURGH
EDINBURGH

# Contents

# Acknowledgements

This book uses data from the 1981 Scottish School Leavers Survey, which was conducted by the Centre for Educational Sociology (CES) at the University of Edinburgh in conjunction with the Scottish Education Department, with support from the Economic and Social Research Council, the Scottish Education Department and the Manpower Services Commission. The help of all these sponsors is gratefully acknowledged.

I am grateful to Margaret MacDougall and Kathy Rogers for processing the writings of the school leavers, and particularly to Margaret MacDougall for her preparation of this volume for phototypesetting. I would thank Pam Armstrong for her assistance and David Stewart-Robinson of the Edinburgh Regional Computing Centre for making the phototypesetter available for our use.

Thanks are also due to my other colleagues at the CES, and particularly Andrew McPherson, for their advice and support.

Our greatest debt is to the school leavers who took the trouble to reply to the questionnaire and to set down what they thought.

# Introduction

In the spring of 1981 questionnaires were sent to a cross-section of leavers from the 1979/80 session in Scottish schools. These young people were taking part in the 1981 Scottish School Leavers Survey, one of a series of surveys conducted by the Centre for Educational Sociology (CES) at Edinburgh University in conjunction with the Scottish Education Department. What the young people's replies indicate about the state of education in Scotland, and about the prospects facing school leavers, may be found in two books. In *Fourteen to Eighteen*, also published in 1984, four members of the CES analyse the information collected in the questionnaires. They discuss the implications of their analyses for current reforms of education and training for the 14-18 age group. The second book based on the 1981 survey is *The Best Years?*. Its authors are the school leavers themselves, and they are left to speak in their own words with a minimum of editorial intervention.

On the back pages of the questionnaires the young people were invited to write about various aspects of their experiences at school and afterwards. This book presents a selection of their replies. It has two parts. The first contains comments that have been selected for their intrinsic interest even though they may not have been representative of the views of the school leavers as a whole. The arrangement of the comments in Part I corresponds to the different topics on which random subsets of the school-leaver sample were invited to comment. It also corresponds, more broadly, to the topics discussed in *Fourteen to Eighteen*. Within each topic the comments have been grouped according to the school leavers' levels of achievement in public examinations. This information, together with the brief biographical details that are given, provides a context for their views.

In Part II a random cross-section of comments, 141 in all, is reproduced in its entirety. They were all responses to the questions used on the back page of version 3 of the questionnaire:

> Would you like to tell us more about yourself? What was
> good about your school? What could be made better?

What has your life been like since leaving school? Has
your school education helped you? Please tell us about
the things that happened at school and after.

The replies were selected randomly and with no regard to their content.
They are grouped into three broad levels of academic achievement but
no other order has been imposed. Readers may wish to read them
*seriatim* or, alternatively, to sample them using the index of topics.

Appendix 2 lists the questions used in Part I as well as in Part II. It
includes all the versions of the questions used on the back pages of the
1981 questionnaire.

The representativeness of the 141 young persons is discussed in
Appendix 1. Readers should note that compared with the population of
school leavers in 1979/80 the group of 141 contains "too many" young
persons with Highers, and "too few" with no certificates at all. The table
in Appendix 1 indicates the scale of any rule-of-thumb adjustment the
reader might make in using the comments from Part II to form an overall
impression of the views of the population of school leavers, as a
questionnaire might elicit them.

How different these views would have been, had they been expressed
through a different medium, is a question that cannot be answered. But
it is perhaps worth bearing in mind that the young people wrote their
comments approximately nine months after they had left school,
addressing them to a researcher whom they would never meet. The only
ostensible incentive to write was the researcher's assurance to them that
their views would be carefully studied and would prove helpful to others.

All allusions to the identity of the writers, their schools, teachers and
places of work, have of course been anonymised. The grammar and
spelling of the originals have been retained.

The presentation of views in *The Best Years?* may be contrasted with
that adopted in an earlier selection of school leavers' writings, *Tell Them
From Me*, published in 1980. In addition to updating the coverage of *Tell
Them From Me*, *The Best Years?* also covers a broader range of young
people. In *Tell Them From Me* special attention was given to the
experiences of young people who left school in the 1970s with few, if any,
academic qualifications. *The Best Years?* includes comments from young
people across the whole range of academic attainment, and it covers a
broader range of issues than were discussed in the earlier book.

Subject to resource constraints, the data from the 1981 survey, like all
the school leavers surveys conducted by the CES, are available for re-
analysis through the Scottish Education Data Archive. This applies both
to the numerical data and, for the 1981 survey alone, to some of the open-
ended comments as well. A much larger selection of comments than that
presented here is available for analysis in machine-readable form. The
anonymity of the respondents has been protected both in the numerical
data and in the comments.

*Fourteen to Eighteen* concluded that current efforts for reform "are in danger of being dissipated if no more rational system can be found for framing the choices of students". *The Best Years?* tells us how the young people themselves viewed their situation, but in their words alone, and not in the words of the researchers, or of the sponsors, or of anyone else.

**References**

Lesley Gow and Andrew McPherson (eds), *Tell Them From Me*, Aberdeen University Press, 1980.
David Raffe (ed.), *Fourteen to Eighteen*, Aberdeen University Press, 1984.

# Part I. Selected Comments

"To begin with I would like to say that I have found filling in this questionnaire very interesting and thought-provoking and hope that my opinions may prove helpful"

## 1. The Perfect School

"This school would be fantastic compared to the school that I went to"

"My school is wasted with vandalism"

"I feel there could never be a perfect school, because everybody has their own views and opinions"

**Non-certificate leavers**

My pefect school would be a .new modern school which is brightly decorated. I would like the school to let you do any subject that would get you the right qualification to get you the job that you were seeking and beable to sit any number of o grades. The teacher should beable to talk to us like a person and not a child and we should beable to talk freely with the teachers about your school work and any problems that you have. I do think that you should go to school because you would never get any where with out being educated. The rules in the school should be fair not to strict and not to lenient.

This school would be fantastic compared to the school that I went to, The school was so cold and dreary and you could not talk freely to the teachers about your school work, and I did not like the way they just past you by because you were not the brightist kid in school. And you had to sit six O grades or sit none at all because the way they grade you, which is mad because if I went to any other school in town you get to sit one o grade if you liked.

> *Female, non-certificate. Shop assistant.*

My perfect school would be like the one I attended, [], with some slight changes, for example, more pupil participation in the running of the school. If a teacher is particularly unpopular and the pupils feel something should be done, a delegation should be able to have a talk or should I say discussion with said teacher. Views would be aired on both sides and hopefully, improvement in relations would occur. Of course there should be rules, no society can survive without them, as pupils it is our duty to attend school. I'm sure we all realise after we have left school how important it was to our development.

In my ideal school I think there should be more discipline rather than the trend nowadays to be lenient.

For pupils with little likelyhood of gaining o grades e.t.c. much more time should be spent in practical tuition than is at present. They, (in our area at least) seem to go out of school a lot and have much more leisure pursuits.

> *Female, non-certificate. On a work experience scheme as a shop assistant in a bakery.*

My school would start at 10.00am too 6.00pm because 8.00am is too early. The school would be a new school and have heated classrooms and decent PE eqipment. The teachers would understand your problems and listen to your ideas. I would do a way with RE and music and bring in something about life after school. Jobs marriage sex etc. You would'nt have to wear school uniforms and you should be able to wear what you want. You have to do aleast three years of schooling at secondry. There would be longer break times. My school would be much better than the school I went too. My old school was to old fashioned you could'nt even come in with dyed hair or a short hair cut.

*Male, non-certificate. On a work experience scheme as a builder.*

My Perfect School would be one which start about 8.00 and finish about 2.30 and you would be able to choose your own subjects and everyone gets on well together. While you were there you would have to work really hard in the Subjects, Join the clubs that were available.

The teachers would get on well with their pupils but they would have to be quite strict because if they weren't the pupils would run riat and disrupt other classes. Yes, You would have to go because If you didn't then you wouldn't have any qualifications, and you wouldn't have a very good change of getting a job also you wouldn't have a very good education.

I think there should be some rules for smoking, drugs, drinking and valdalising but I don't think it is Important to have rules for School Uniform etc.

My Ideal School compares a lot better than the School I went to because the house blocks were always in a mess, there were people smoking in the toilets also the toilets were vandalised, there was always someone in a fight, there was rules for everything, the teachers were quite strict.

*Female, non-certificate. Taking a full-time course (unspecified).*

1.   A strict headmaster but understanding
2.   Girls can wear trousers
3.   No vanalisim
4.   A good youth Wing
5.   Sombody if in trouble you can talk to freely
6.   Better equipment and materials
7.   At PE pick what you would like to do and not be forced into a sport you dislike.
8.   Teachers to be friendly and more understanding and to treat you more like an adult and not to look down on you as if you were dirt.
9.   I would do some subjects but most of all I would like to trampolining and swim all day about three whole days out of the week

My ideal school is not like the [] the teachers can really be very hurtful when not nessaserry. My school is wasted with vandalism. The swimming pool is very dirty at time with scum and dirt I would have it well looked after. The headmaster is the way I would like it. PE is terrible the teachers pick what you've to do and if you refuse your belted which its terrible if you really have a dislike to the game.

The teachers still treat you as a child sometimes and say right [] get out of here I am on the reprographic machine I just say sorry but I am booked in and have a long run but most teachers are all right.

> *Female, non-certificate. On a work experience scheme as a community assistant.*

## O grade leavers

My idea of a perfect school would be one that gave you subjects you enjoyed and would be of use to you.

I would also like the teachers to treat us with more respect and intelligence instead of looking upon us as an inferior race, how are we supposed to treat them with respect when it is not returned and appreciated, I would like to go to a school that the teachers made an effort to communicate with you.

I think they shouldn't give you subjects like history, geography, science etc they may be quite intresting to some people, I liked history at school, but they are not practical and do not prepare you for life outside school; I think you should be prepared for looking for jobs what to expect etc from 1st yr at school in this day and age and with the mess our country is in it is about the most sensible thing to do.

> *Female, O grades, no A-C awards. Unemployed and not looking for work.*

I feel there could never be a perfect school, because everybody has their own views and opinions. What my perfect school would be like:

> Good teachers, knew how to teach their subjects.
> Strict but pleasant and fun teachers
> you would have to go for lessons but not to library,
> study classes,
> free periods,
> alternative classes eg PE, Religious Education *if* you didn't want to.
> Yes there would have to be rules, as it would be hopeless to run a school with out them.

My school was a good school, they teachers (almost all) were pleasant and strict. Some rules I did not agree with such as minor things like 'no one allowed in the rooms during break', and 'no walking along corridors, go outside and in the entrance for your class.'

We were made to go to library classes etc. – I disagree with that. You don't realise till you leave that school times are the happiest times in all your life. I feel there should have been more told to us about the outside world (once you leave school) alcohol, drugs, sex etc. We were told very little, and these are *very very* important. I enjoyed answering your survey.

> *Female, O grades. Doing a medical secretarial course at an FE college.*

My perfect school is just like the college I am at now, as there is more freedom and teachers do not pull you down in front of the class. Of course there has to be rules to keep everything in order and keep things running smoothly, and everyone to obey these rules or the school would be kiosk.

As for the teachers, are much better at college than school as they are more friendlier and down to earth. But at my school some of the teaches were too high and mighty and they looked down on you as just people that were there to learn work. More facilities for teenagers at school when they go to PE, and they can select what they want to do. Not just to be told to go to a hall and get on with a game everyone hates as this is not much fun for us when we only got 2 periods of it a week.

As for some of the subjects I took I was shoved into different classes or given unknown teachers and this of course had dropped the time and education of the subject because of teachers illness. I think there should be a teacher ready to take the position and not to disturb the education of pupils during 4th year.

> *Female, O grades, no A-C awards. Taking a full-time course at an FE college.*

I have no idea of a perfect school as there never will or can be one. Also it is usually not the school that is at fault but the teachers pupils who attend it. Therefore I was perfectly happy at the school I was at and in my opinion no other school can beat it.

> *Female, O grades. Bank clerkess.*

**Highers leavers**

My perfect school would be much like the one I went to. However several improvements could be made. There could be a better pupil-teacher relationship, especially between older teachers and pupils. Pupils should once again be given some kind of incentive to do well both at academic and sports activities. Dicipline would be strict but punishment would only be administered in severe cases. Any punishment administered would have some relevence to the crime commited instead of corporal punishment and lines. Pupils would also be given more career information to prepare them more fully for going out into the world. They would also be told that unemployment is a fact of life that they may have to live with. School would still be compulsory.
*Female, Highers. Bank clerkess.*

The school which I attended was not far removed from being my ideal school.
Facilities were more than adequate and also open to the public during holiday periods e.g. swimming pool, sports ground, leisure room. I find this a particularly good idea as I live in an area, lacking in such amenities.
I would like to have a place at school were students would be able to study after school hours especially towards exam time, I find it difficult to study at home as I am constantly interrupted, I am sure many other students share this problem. I think teachers could be more encouraging to those pupils with less than a 'special aptitude' for their particular subject. School and university is primarily a place of learning and study over a period of time therefore I am against exams in school and university – a days work which will determine a students future. The person concerned should be marked according to the standard of work achieved throughout the year and then merited accordingly. Hopefully in the near future all schools will become better equipped with facilities – more teachers – smaller classes, so that everyone a better and equal standard of education – regardless of social class. This will create not only a better society but also a better future for generations to come.
*Female, Highers. Studying languages at university.*

School should become less of an institution – more cooperation should be involved. Less dogmatism & unquestioned authority. Outside inspection of working of school should be employed more regularly & thoroughly. Extra-curricular activities must be provided to keep students or scholars interested in their school. The present system drives pupils to resentment, and I, for one, felt constraint in my relationship with teachers due to their position of authority – their cliqueish profession indulges their delusions of superiority, manifested in their condescending manner.

*Female, Highers. Studying law at university.*

My ideal school would firstly involve more money being spent, especially to get several small computers for pupils' (and teachers') use. More use should be made of school buildings in the evenings – not just sports facilities, but cheap hire of rooms for clubs, political societies, etc. and possibly a coffee bar/cafe for use of teachers and pupils. If properly run this could actually make money (though not by charging dear prices), and more importantly if used by teachers as well, it would let pupils get to know their teachers and create better relations.

More responsibility should be given to pupils, expecially older ones. Ridiculous bans on certain items of clothing (e.g. denims) should be removed, and school uniform should not be obligatory. Also no pupil who has passed leaving age should be asked for a note covering absence, or given corporal punishment. Pupils should be encouraged to take an interest in the running of the school, and an elected council given some powers (I was member of one in 5th year which had no powers whatsoever, was ignored, and collapsed after everyone realised the farce it was).

Religious education should be limited to comparative studies, and segregated schools (religious and sexual) abolished. It would be a good idea to have political lessons and discussions. All pupils (male and female) should be taught woodwork/sewing/cookery etc. Finally, more toleration of unorthodox teachers should be shown by the teaching establishment.

*Male, Highers. Studying computing at university.*

## 2. School in Third and Fourth Years

"I think that you should be taught
how to spell better in schools and
how to wright"

"they walk away thinking that you
understand"

"I did not need O'levels for my job,
but I am glad that I sat them"

"I think the school curriculum has
alot of unnecessary subjects in it"

**Non-certificate leavers**

We never got asked to do o levels, o grades or prelims. Yes I did want to sit the O grade exam.
In a non-Certificate class you had to do the Subjets that they picked for you we got no choice in anything, which I think is very unfair becouse we could at least try them if we failed them at least we had a chance to to them. we never got the choice to do or say anything about it.
*Female, non-certificate. Works in a clothing factory.*

There was nothing to do in non-Certificale Classes.
*Female, non-certificate. On a work experience scheme as a shop assistant in a greengrocer.*

**O grade leavers**

1/ I think there has got to be a system of new classes which teache you how to cope with such things as interviews, taxforms, benefits and how to deal with money.
2/ I think careers officers are a waste of time, they did nothing to help me and in some ways they hindered me. We should teach youngsters and teenagers to write more neatly and to spell. Also to read with confidance. What is the use of knowing the inside of the alimentary tract, when you can't write or spell and you don't have the confidance to check copy with your fellow workers?
*Female, O grades. Assistant in advertising agency.*

The one thing I didn't like about school was there was too big a jump in the work from 2nd year to 3rd year. I was able to cope with the work in 2nd year, but in 3rd year I was completely lost. I think they could spread the work out a little more. I thought my courses at school were very interesting and the teachers always tried to make them as interesting as possible. There was always plenty of time to study in school, but I didn't take advantage of it. At my school the teachers tried to help you, they knew what you were capable of.
*Female, O grades. Taking a full-time secretarial course at an FE college.*

I think if they started Fourth year work in *third* year it would be easier to pass your 'o' grades because I didn't think any third year work was asked about in your 'o' grade exams so your third year was wasted as it could have been used to study work that would be more useful in your 'o' grade exams. Our music teacher [] was *fantastic!* she ran a choir which we attended once a week which I really enjoyed very much. She put on a play each year which was always very good and everyone enjoyed both the audience and all the people who took part especially [our music teacher].

    *Female, O grades. Shop assistant.*


If I was good at a subject my teachers would encourage me but if I was not so good I got no encouragement, my parents were advised to let me take the o-levels I did and did not have the experience of a child at o-level stages and thought this was good advice, but it turned out the o-levels I took did not encourge job prospects. So I would advise teachers to really find out what a child wants to do before giving their advice. I have personel experience of going job hunting and there is too much put on o-levels and highers. My parents had no o-levels and both are well educated people who have worked in industry all there lives. I think o-levls should either be well controlled or scrapped. PS. It has taken me all my time to answer this as I feel so strongly about it.

    *Male, O grades. Tiler.*


I think that you should be taught how to spell better in schools and how to wright and pronounce the words the way they should be. While doing English in my last two years of School the teachers were reading to us from books and it was the same period after period and most people got fed up listening and just gave up. I know Primary School taught you how to spell, but not the kind of words that are essential when writing for jobs etc., I found the last two years of school very boring as you were being taught the same things over again instead of new and different things to give you more knowledge of the subject.

My school education has helped me since I left school because if I could not type I would not have the job I am in at the moment. I did not need O'levels for my job, but I am glad that I sat them, even although I only passed one O'level, it was the self satisfaction of passing one that I didn't take much interest in until two days before sitting the O'level. I studied more with my other two subject, but failed.

I think my biggest problem was when doing exams, not just O'levels all exams, you come up against some long words and you do not know the meaning of them, as you were never taught them, when you asked a teacher the meaning of the word they explain it with even more long words and walk away thinking that you understand.

These are my own personal views on school, I know they are mostly on spelling but I do think this is very important. P.S. Sorry for delay in replying.

*Female, 1 O grade. Clerical assistant/typist.*

O-grades are a good way to assess work, yet I think I am not alone in saying that a fairer way to establish qualifications would be to have some sort of assessment system based on the whole year's work, attendance and written class tests. There is a lot of lost sleep and worry over O-grades and this makes the performance of the pupil rather lower perhaps than what he or she normally does.

I think the school curriculum has alot of unnecessary subjects in it – eg. Algebra, P.E, R.E. Subjects such as Physical Education and Religious Education should not be made compulsory but each individual should have a choice of doing these subjects or opting out

Many pupils opt for truancy rather than face these undesirable subjects.

*Female, O grades. Stayed in Fifth year to study six Highers, but left before taking examinations. On a work experience scheme as a library assistant.*

I regret not doing well in school. I wanted to go into the WRAF in Electronics But when sceince is classed as a boys subject I didn't have a chance. I now want to work with children as a Mothers help/Nanny.

*Female, O grades, no A-C awards. Unemployed.*

I think at that age you dont realisle how Important it is to Study and obtain good Results in the exams. The future and a Job seem years away. We went into third year and had to choose what Subjects we wanted to study for the O'grades. I think what went wrong there was, that alot of School kids are too young to make a decision like that, which will effect thier whole future. Maybbay Some arent. But most people I knew and alot of my friends Just choose the Subjects which they *Liked!* and not what they would need for thier future career. As at that time hardly anyone knew what they wanted to do. I didnt know myself either.

*Female, O grades. Unemployed.*

**Highers leavers**

The exam system just now is not satisfactory because to pass an exam you do not have to understand the subject you merely have to "swot" up the relevant information and produce it in a parrot like fashion in the exams this is especially true in regards to "O" grades.

*Male, Highers. Studying quantity surveying at an FE college.*

## 3.  Leaving at Christmas

"Nobody could careless if you went
to school or not"

"It was like as thou we were Thrown
aside from the rest of the school and
forgoten about"

## Non-certificate leavers

I left school at christmas. I missed all my friends I useto run around with and all the teacher's I had for my subjects. And then I began to wish I was back at school and now I would do anything to turn the clock's back so that I could go back to school.

> *Male, non-certificate. Electrical linesman.*

I left school at Christmas and at that time it was good for christmas leavers because the teachers were more cheary because of the festivaties and christmas thoughts. At my school every year at christmas the music department and english department came together and mad a concert, teachers and pupils alike. The money we gaind from the ticket selling went to funds to help the school in many ways, but the christmas festivitys did not always bring happienes as windows were brocken with stones consealed in snow balls. There were long lectures afterwards to try and prevent it happening again but this did not help which ended in partisapents in this vandalistic pass time bieng suspended.

> *Male, non-certificate. Sales assistant.*

It was worthwile leaving at Christmas for those who were not sitting any exams.

> *Female, non-certificate. Unemployed.*

I especially liked the xmas leaving course which was very interesting, as we visited factory's and different places and fotnd out what work world be like, when we left school.

> *Female, non-certificate. On a work experience scheme in a factory.*

Dear Madame, To tell the truth the last year at school could have been more useful than it turned out, for the fact is when your teachers find out that you are leaving at christmas, you would be just as well not being there. You get taken out of the lessons that you are interested in and end up with lessons that would be no good to anyone. Nobody could careless if you went to school or not.

> *Female, non-certificate. Office junior.*

I left school at christmas and I do not regret leaving school as I have a very good job and had I stayed on at School to do my O'Levels I would not have got the job. I enjoyed school very much but the last four months were terrible, you were moved from class to class with nothing to do you, always got graded as a "Christmas Leaver". But since I left school they have started a whole new system with the future school leavers. In the last few months of school we were all put into one class there was about seventeen christmas leavers and called "5R". We got a timetable which was full of subject half the class hadn't even taken before, and put into classes with the Fourth Years. It was the worst time of my whole school life as we were not treated as normal school leavers nor Pupils.

> *Female, non-certificate. Trainee dispenser (chemist).*

I left school at christmas and I think it was a waste of time being cept on because I thout That we didnt seem to learn anay more. It was like as thou we were Thrown aside from the rest of the school and forgoten about. Nearer the end of Term I stayed of To go out and look for A Job. But it wasent long before I got called back For Playing Trewent. The subjects I was in in the my last year – were a waste of time because we didnt learn anything more. We were just sitting doing more or less the same sort of things as we had a ready learnt. I think christmas leavers – should be given Time of to get A chance to look For employment before they leave school – to give them A A chance.

> *Male, non-certificate. On a work experience scheme as a tyre fitter.*

I left in May. There were only one boy in our class that left at christmas after us and he didnot like when he was still there, and we were all away.

> *Male (summer leaver), non-certificate. Unemployed.*

## O grade leavers

I left school at Christmas and thought that for those leaving at this time of year it was a disgrace at the way we had to sit about in classes with almost nothing to do, because the teachers weren't interested in you because you were not staying or for Highers. Some days it was alright if you were at an activities group like helping with the play group, o.a.p.'s afternoon etc, but most of the time you just had to sit and be bored. I think that it is about time something was done about those who have to stay on for a part of Fifth Year.

*Female, O grades. Clerkess in music shop.*

I left school at Christmas Because I was too young to Leave at Summer but 5th year was enjoyable Because is was more LEISURALLY and interesting than the first 4 year. In 5th year we went on educational trips at work sites to study the routine of employment.

*Male, O grades. Metal stripper in scrap yard.*

I left school at Christmas 1979 and from July 79 to December 79 school was just boring we did nothing in class just talk between ourselves.

*Male, O grades, no A-C awards. Apprentice electrican.*

I think it is silly that people who want to leave school, are held on till Christmas because they are not old enough. It would be better to let them leave school because they aren't going to be interested in school from Summer up until Christmas when they eventually leave.

*Male, O grades. Taking a business studies course.*

# 4. School in Fifth and Sixth Years

"the step from O'level to higher
exams is much larger than you
think"

"The respectibility is falling away
from the younger generation
nowadays, and no wonder"

"its very hard to be 'creative' under
forced conditions of time &
environment"

My fifth and sixth years at school were thoroughly enjoyable, although as far as qualifications go, they were two completely wasted years. – I wouldn't have missed them for the world, or changed them in any way.

By the time I reached 5th & 6th year, I felt a lot closer to the staff, and began looking at them as ordinary people! By sixth year especially, the majority were more like friends & classes were much more informal

Although my 5th & 6th year results were not good, I would not blame this on the more relaxed and informal relationships, but on my own attitude.

So far, my school education hasn't helped a lot, since I'm in a job requiring no qualifications, but I think it will in time to come, e.g. if I go to Bible College. I think it is essential for everyone to gain as many qualifications from school as possible. I know that the job situation is bad & I know the attitude of some people toward studying is "what's the point, it doesn't guarantee a job". It's true of course, that it doesn't, but if prospects with qualifications are bleak, then it should be obvious its not on to hope for a decent job without.

> *Female, Highers. Nursing auxillary. Conditional acceptance to do business studies at university.*

In fifth year I sat four highers & 1 O'level, I did not pass one of my highers, which after passing six O'levels the year before (3A's,B,2 C's) not only disappointed my family & myself but also surprised us. I have several reasons for this, two of which are more important than the others. (1) I do not think that it is explained clearly enough or even emphasised enough that the step from O'level to higher exams is much larger than you think. After all you have at the very least two years to prepare for an O'level, but only one for a higher exam. I think that this was a very important detail that should never have been under emphasised thus luring us into a false sense of security. (2) My second reason is a much more personal reason in that I think I was unlucky with my teachers. I do not wish to use the excuse that mine were any less competent than others but merely that three out of the four teachers that taught me at higher level were heads' of their particular department. I do not believe that the head of a department should be teaching at higher level as their is little enough time to squeeze in the necessary information that is needed to pass a higher exam into one lesson without the interuptions that inevitably happen. All too frequently my teachers were called to meetings out with the school, within the school, or called to solve problems within his/her own department. All these things wasted precious time. All this doesn't matter if you can work on & on, on your own, but many of us find we are stuck at small problems which, had the teacher been there, could have been solved quickly allowing us to go on

with our work. My fourth Higher teacher left after the first term & was
not replaced until the following year, once the exams were over.
*Female, Highers. Library assistant.*


I thought Higher English was more interesting than 'O' grade English.
The Higher exam however wasn't as 'worthwhile' – its very hard to be
'creative' under forced conditions of time & environment e.g. for the
composition. I think there could be more book/poem analysis in the
course (similar to S.Y.S) and less emphasis put on the "interpretations"
which I think are stressed too much. I think a more mature approach to
the exam could be considered. I think pupils would benefit more by
critical analysis of more books as opposed to much time being spent on
improving your 'interpretation' technique.
Often the whole year was geared for the exam (necessarily but not of
teachers' design) and you worked for the exam during the year. In
Geography we were mostly taught by answering exam questions (or
questions similar to.) Often practical work had to be neglected because
of shortage of time. Because this is not examinable it is the obvious thing
to leave out which is a pity because chemistry *is* a practical subject & so
is Physics. The teachers would have liked to have done more but time
didn't allow.
I think the teachers made my school better than most – they were
prepared to give up spare time etc. to attend to pupils' needs.
*Male, Highers. Studying chemistry at university.*


Facilities at the school [] very poor. It was a very old school, which was
divided into three different parts, a lot of wasted time travelling from
place to place for each class.
The subjects I studied in fifth year were interesting for me, as I really
enjoyed art and History, + also English. If you kept up with your work
steadily, the amount of time before exams was about right.
As I passed only two of my highers, I had to return to school for a sixth
year, only to find I had to repeat my fifth year over again. I didn't agree
with this, as I was made to take subjects I didn't want to do, just to fill
up my timetable. This meant I had less time to study for the subjects I
really needed, no free time at all, and no sixth year privelagees e.g. not
allowed in their common room. It also meant you lost most of your
former friends who were in your classes before, and put in with younger
people, who had their own friends as well. It made me feel quite lonely,
and also embarrassed. At the end of fifth year repeat, it was worth it as
I aquired the subjects I needed to enter Art College.

I am sorry I have been so long, in answering this questionnaire, but recently I have had a lot of work to cope with, because of my assessments.
*Female, Highers. Taking a full time general course at art college.*

I feel O levels should be sat perhaps in 3rd year and more time should be spent on Higher work perhaps taking two years to study to the appropriate level because I feel the teaching for Highers is too exam motivated. We only seem to be taught things which might come up in the exams and so the subject is limited. There is also far too great a jump to be covered properly between Higher and 'O' level in one year.
I also found a great difference in the French taught at University and the French we were expected to know on going to University than what we did at school and wondered why we were not taught the same French in University as in school
I feel that schools ought to have a better system for giving homework because some evenings I had no homework in 5th year and then on other evenings several teachers gave out homework therefore I had to sit on occasions for up to 4 hours doing homework. But perhaps this was just my school which didn't have a very good system.
*Female, Highers. Doing French studies at university.*

If you only intended going straight to University then school obviously helps in that it gets you the qualifications necessary – how much it helped the unemployed person I don't know. I found sixth year a frustrating waste of time after having been subjected to the usual "SYS is the best preparation for university" con. Nevertheless it was essential for *one* higher – someone failed to inform me (despite interviews) that a higher chemistry was necessary for my course – had I known this I could have done it in fifth year. Perhaps encouraging the individual to go and find these things out for themselves is the solution, and this could have been done by the "Careers Officers" rather than just looking at your marks and dismissing you with a "you're allright" and you foolishly believing him.
Also, having concentrated on sciences, I wish that there had been some sort of compulsory lessons on "the world around us" i.e. some politics/ social studies. Yrs moaningly,
*Male, Highers. Studying biology at university.*

There was good aspects about the school I went to. Because it was a Comprehensive, I met people from different social backgrounds, far more than I would have if I had gone to Private school.

The teaching of the subjects was not good. This was evident, when I started doing Higher subjects. The teacher had to get through a fixed amount of work in a short time and this made the understanding and enjoyment of the subjects, less favourable for us. It couldn't have been too enjoyable for the teachers either. I feel I would have got more from a subject if the pace was slowed down and if there was less pressure on us.

I am opposed to sitting examinations. I was sitting highers at the age of 16 and I think that was too young to sit highers. I think that continuos assessment is a better idea. It would have to be properly organized. I'm not sure individual school assessment is a good idea.

The amount which had to be learned for a higher topic is unfair on the pupil. A lot of ground has to be covered in eight months and if a person is sitting quite a few highers, the pressure in comparison to O'levels comes as quite a shock. I noticed this in 5th year. I think the way we were prepared for this exams was also wrong. In Fourth year we finished the work for all subjects at December, when we sat the estimates. This gave us six months to go over all the work again, so if you paid attention at did some work at home. When you do highers, it is basically up to yourself, and although independence is a good idea, its difficult to change like that, if you have been spoon-fed before.

My school career has helped me in some ways, but a lot of problems have arisen since I left school and went to college. I have had to do most of the work if not all on my own, and the level of difficulty has increased. I do think that people going to school after me, should find the subjects more interesting and enjoyable. I felt I did not get so much enjoyment as I had expected and the latter years of my time at school was less enjoyable because the work became less interesting and because of the large amount of work to be done, just before the exams.

*Male, Highers. Doing business studies at an FE college.*


My main complaint about school is that I was forced to waste too much time in my first four years. Studying for O-grades did not tax my abilities and I became very lazy, expecting that I could just sit back and pass exams without working for them. The sudden change in standard between O-grade and higher work came as a surprise and I found it very difficult to discipline myself to work. If I had been allowed to work at my own pace I could have passed O grade exams in second year and spent the next three years doing something more profitable. This way the transition from O-grade to higher would not have seemed so difficult and since I would have been used to working I could have obtained much better grades at Higher. There would also have been much more time to spend studying for higher exams and I could have taken a wider range of subjects. I was lucky to have exceptionally good teachers for all but one of my subjects in fifth year, especially my chemistry teacher whom I felt I could look upon as a friend. If schools were carefull to select only those teachers who had as much enthusiasm, dedication and genuine concern for their pupils *as individuals* as he had then the population in general would be better educated.

The guidance staff at my school did try to do their best, but in such a large school even their best wasn't very much. You were considered to be lucky if a member of the guidance staff could even remember your name, and so they could not possibly be expected to give advice on careers, because to be able to do this with any degree of success demands that the advisor knows the personality and background of the pupil very thoroughly. With such a small ratio of guidance staff to pupils in my school the guidance system is useless. A much better method would be to assign each pupil in the school to a particular teacher who would act as an informal councillor, much the same as the student councillor schemes in operation in many universities. I personally found that I could get much more sound advice from the few teachers whose classes I had attended through each of the five years at high school because they knew me as a person and not just another kid in the same school uniform. To employ people for this sole purpose is a mistake because it is only an exceptional teacher who will not look upon it simply and impersonally as a job of work and each pupil becomes just another file to be tidied away. Teachers can only be expected to know and therefore to give advice to those pupils who move in and out of their classrooms every day and because of this their opinions are much more valuable than those of the guidance staff whose function seems to be mainly administrational. *All* good teachers should be expected to give guidance to their pupils on any relevant topic – if teachers were more thoughtfully trained and more carefully selected then there would be no need for 'guidance' staff.

Schools should teach pupils things like how to fill out application forms, what their rights as employees are, how much they should expect to pay in income tax, national insurance, superannuation, pension funds etc, how to claim unemployment, supplementary and sickness benefits, what p45's & p60's are, how current and deposit bank accounts are run, how to budget wages to keep a home and what their civil rights are. How can any system possibly claim to educate its pupils when they leave school with practically no knowledge of such things which will certainly be an integral part of their lives for a very long time. Education on politics, the importance of trade unions, voting, sex and child rearing and social dangers such as V.D, alcohol, cigarettes and drugs should also be provided.

*Female, Highers. Studying pharmacy at university.*

You question me about smoking and drinking being health problems. Well I noticed in my last year at school that these two problems along with drugs and glue sniffing were creeping into the school scene. In my school alone, a number of girls were treated for taking Valium, a number of guys for sniffing glue, smoking is no longer forbidden in the school, and discos and parties are only drunken brawls. The respectibility is falling away from the younger generation nowadays, and no wonder. Something is needing to be done. School activities? Could they help? we don't know unless they are given a try. But we can't afford to just have something for the minority to take part in. The range has got to cover everything even boxing for the "hard-men" and "glue sniffers" etc and once we get things going it's got to be kept that way. Taming the animals!

> *Male, Highers. Laboratory technician, hoping to go to an FE college.*

A balanced Arts/science type of course should be recomended for sixth year students intending University taking perhaps 1-2 SYS subjects in their intended field of study and some other combination of subjects totally unrelated which they perhaps have not studied before. An exclusive diet of related science SYS subjects stifles intellectual development and crushes an inquiring mind with its excessive factual knowledge recall basis.

Studying a subject for its own sake when the student is mature enough to appretiate it – as against early in the school life – leads to a more open minded individual more appreciative of other peoples intrests, and philosophies.

> *Male, Highers. Studying medicine at university.*

*English:* While literature counts for 37.5 per cent of the Higher and 20 per cent of the "O"-grade exams, over 90 per cent of class time in years 4 & 5 was spent on literature. More time should have been spent on other aspects of English. *Practical Work*: In principle, S.Y.S. projects (Chemistry & Physics) are a very good idea, but there are problems. Different schools have different quantities and quality of equipment (Some excellent, some abysmal) and different levels of enthusiasm and ability in their S.Y.S. teachers (this makes a great difference). It may also occur that an able pupil (practically & theoretically) may try an ambitious project which involves some risk as to whether or not good results are obtained while a less able pupil may try a less ambitious project which is practically guaranteed to give good results.

As a result of all these factors, the mark received for a project may not reflect a pupil's ability to do a practical project. Personally, I found that practical experience gained working for [an electronics firm] in June-September 1980 was of much more benefit than C.S.Y.S. projects.

*Usefulness of a 6th Year (especially C.S.Y.S.)* In my opinion, my own 6th year (In which I did only C.S.Y.S.) was worthwhile, and most pupils intending to go to university *can* benefit from doing C.S.Y.S. However, in too many cases this either does not happen or cannot happen.

I know of people who have tried to do a C.S.Y.S. course and would have benefited from it, but their school would not or could not provide the time, teachers or equipment. (In one case the S.Y.S. courses were run as evening classes).

I also know of people who have been given every opportunity to do a worthwhile S.Y.S. course, but have finished up by making no effort at all in their courses, allowing their marks to slump and generally wasting their time.

This problem of making a 6th year worthwhile could be largely solved by making better use of existing resources (see above paragraph).

*Career's Service* Some Careers Service Inspectors once came to the school to discuss the career's service with pupils. For over an hour, they talked about people, books and services that we had, for the most part, never heard of. 'Nuff said? (I exempt one teacher [] who is very helpful and useful, but only if you can find him first.)

> *Male, Highers. Studying electronics at university.*

## 5.   Their Own School...

"Money can buy pratictly anything,
but it can't buy happiness like I had
at school"

"Since leaving school I seem to have
learned more than I did in my last
year"

**Non-certificate leavers**

I won't be suprised if you can't read my writting but anyway I realy liked school a lot, I never even missed half a day for the four years I was at secondary school.

The very first day after the Christmas Hollidays I wished I hadn't left school. I wished I was back at school even up to my first real job. You see every body wouldn't dream of washing dishes for a living, and it's certainly the last job I had in mind when I left school. But for seventy pound a week, it's worth it, but after you are eighteen you get promoted to an assistant cook, with double the money.

Money can buy pratictly anything, but it can't buy happiness like I had at school. Don't get me wrong I am happy, but it's not the same as when I was at school. As far as I'm conserned my school was the only school. I got on great with all the teacher's not to mention the pupil's and I suppose your wondering why I left school so early and to give up my "O" levels for a job wich I never even got, well I gues you think your old enough to decied for yourself. Everybody tells you not to leave but you think your different and wont miss the school but you do. And soon realise just how many friend's you have lost. Some that you would'nt even speak to when you were at school but would be only to pleased to speak to them now.

Well like I said I only hope you can read my writting but believe me my writting has no reflection what so ever on my school.

*Male, non-certificate. Catering boy on ferry.*

The school I went to was not very good. I went to [], before that I went to [] it was alot better, because, when boys are in your class, I found that I had to much carryon in my head, and at my old school there was no boys. The worse thing about school was it was not near home, and you were not allowed to wear trousers in the winter, plus I dont agree there should be prefects, as you cant do anything, like in the winter they are allowed to stand in corroddors which we had to stand out side, they are there to learn not to be like teachers telling us what to do, as they are only one or two years older, The subjects I took in school, were no help when I left, because, maths and arithmetic, all I think you really need to know is how to count, you dont need fractions, or anything else. English all you need is to talk properly and beable to write and spell, not compositions or Literture, you dont need that when you work. I think you should beable to leave school at fifteen, as when you try to get a job most places they are looking for people with experience, and how can you get that if you are still at school. I think in our school it should never had been mixed, you never learned much, in Arithmetic, all the teacher would say was get a book out and start writing, instead of him taking his time and showing us what to do. I never liked anything about school all I ever wanted to do was get out and try and find a job, probably because I was at [] I lost interest when I went to that school. I think the teachers could help us more to be patient, when it comes to people who are slower than others at learning I think quite a few teachers only where bothered about when it was time to go home.. I think the best thing I ever done was leave school and being so lucky to get a job.

*Female, non-certificate. Receptionist.*

Since leaving school I seem to have learned more than I did in my last year. Fortunately for me I was only one week unemployed. I have now been working for more than a year as a trainee confectioner and I like doing it very much. I have one day a week at the Technical College. I did not like schools all that much but I did my best. I did not stay to try to pass any exams as I was not interested enough and I felt my time was being wasted. I now feel I am learning something that will help me in later years. As for my school education helping me I suppose it must have done some good but at the moment I cannot honestly say it has. The problem as I saw it was if you were one of the lucky ones who sailed through their subjects without any trouble, they seemed to get all the tuition and the people like myself who were that bit slower were left to get on with it.

*Female, non-certificate. Trainee confectioner.*

I found school very boring and when I could I had days off to work on the farm on which I stay. When I found out I was in the thick classes I just gave up because no hope of O'grades. When in fourth year we never got any school trips but the briany ones did which I think is very daft. The only thing that has helped me is how to count and speak. When I left school and started work I thought it was great.

*Male, non-certificate. Carpet fitter.*

I think that the none O grade classes should get more help as they are come out of school knowing nothing.
The classes are to big for people like me who where average but they could better them by making the number young people in a class small. The school leaven age should go up to the age of 17 year.

*Male, non-certificate. On an engineering course at an FE college.*

Our School was friendly. You could get on well with teachers. There were clubs you go to Such as The Drama club, Badminton, Netball, Hockey, Stamp collecting, Gymnastics etc. The rules of the School could be improved and made more stricter. I liked most of the Subjects I studied. I'd like to think they have helped me. At our School we had DRAMA Concerts and Folk Concerts and also Talent Contests. We had discos to raise money for School Strips etc. We also adopted a baby. As the mother was very young and wasn't well off. And at first she wasn't going to have it. Lots of Schools have helped young mothers and their babies like we have. We have ANTI-ABORTIONIST meetings and there we are told about the mothers reasons for not wanting her child. But we never get told the mother's name or anything about her. As she would be probably very embarraced. We bought the baby a pram, nappies, clothes and covers etc. The mother was very pleased and showed her thanks by bringing the baby up to visit.

*Female, non-certificate. Unemployed.*

Dear Sir/madam I do not like writing but I will do the best I can to explain about my-self I did not like my Secondry School but there were some things good about it. I Liked being able to get to know more poeple but some poeple are lost because its so big I think my school education was ok but some subjects dont get you any were but I think it helped me to get on with poeple and help in the house with cooking cleaning and sewing. I left school at christmas and i dont think theres anything for anyone to do so I will close for no.

*Female, non-certificate. Unemployed.*

**O grade leavers**

In my opinion if you do to many courses at school at one time, you stand a greater risk of failing most of them because there are to many.
At my school, I was more than please with the views and attitudes of all the staff.
To sum up. All pupils have a mind of there own and the should be the ones who make up there mind wheather to stay at school or leave it. This decision should be made by them and only them. The same applys with college courses.
SCHOOLS & COLLEGES ARE THERE FOR A PURPOSE! TO OBTAIN & COLLECT EVERY EXAM PASS YOU CAN AFTER

ALL YOU ARE ONE THAT BENEFITS WHEN LOOKING FOR A
CAREER AFTER SCHOOL. THANK YOU VERY MUCH
*Male, O grades. On a work experience scheme with a District
Council.*

My school was very modern and well equipped. The teachers were very
pleasant, who treated us as adults. I don't think there could be any
changes, to make it better. My education hasn't done very much for me.
I was very interested in my 'O'grade subjects. I enjoyed Biology and
French most of all. Yes, they were very interesting, not very useful. Yes,
I enjoyed my lessons. No, I would have liked to have had longer, amount
of time.
At my school, we were always treated like adults. We had special days
to use the library at our leisure. We had regular inspectors in school and
vistors from foreign countries. Alot of activity at lunchtime and after
school, was arranged. We entered alot of competitions. A few shows
were put on. Everything was just great at school. I'am not sorry I left,
I have become more independant, and that was one of my main aims after
leaving school. I'am very grateful to you for including me in your survey.
I have answered it, to my fullest. I hope my information will help you
in your survey. Thank you!
*Female, O grades. Waitress.*

The good things about our school are, there were always plenty of things
to do. As well as going for lessons, it also had many clubs of all different
kinds to go too during breaks and after school such as drama, music,
chess, stamp, fishing photography, badmington, football clubs and many
more. we also had a Scripture union group which I attended. I was the
school Council representative for our school. At the Council we arranged
many inter school competitions for the local schools which helped pupils
from different schools to meet. There were also plenty of outings
arranged for the pupils of our school.
My school Education has helped me since I left school, especially my
geography as the information I learned in the class has helped me with
my farming job. Most of the other subjects I studied at school helped me
aswell although some of the information the teachers give us in certain
subjects is irrelevant and a waste of time.
We had a talking newspaper made up in our school for the local blind
people. I was involved in this. I also went to old folks huts and holmes
and hospitals with other pupils and teachers to entertain them during the
winter. The shool also has a band which has about 40 members. I played

the base tuba in the band. We held many band concerts in the school and local halls and we played at the local church at Christmas and Easter every year.

*Male, O grades. On a work experience scheme as a trainee farmer.*

I didn't like the school much, the teachers weren't much use or good to get on with, although there were some teachers in subjects I was advised not to take that I got on good with and were more use to me than my guidance teacher, careers officers, or any of my 'O' grade subject teachers. My school education wasn't any use to me as I wasn't much interested in the subjects I was taking at school, therefore I didn't bother listening to them or learning them, so I failed [some of] my 'O' grades, a change of my teachers half way during my course wasn't any good for me either, it just made me worse. The courses that I studied in my last year at school were completely the wrong choice (they were advised to me by my guidance teacher) I done better in my non-'O' grade subjects. I wished I had left the school at Christmas, as I was completely bored till 'O' grades & leaving date it made me feel worse altogether. Our school was quite a bad school, their way of dealing with bad behaviour was pathetic, you either got expelled or the belt, (which you got that used, to, it didn't bother you after a while). The teachers werne't much good for talking to, and their advise was totally wrong, I was told that a factory job would be no good to me (by my guidance & careers officer) & I wouldn't last a week there, but I have been in factory for about 1 year now, & I wouldn't change it for anything, the people are great to get on with, & conditions of work are great, my pay is stable and I am much happier now than any of my school years.

*Female, O grades. Machinist in textile industry.*

**Highers leavers**

I liked the friendly atmosphere at my school. The teachers were very helpful and treated you as an equal adult not a sillly child. The facilities in school could be made better for certain subjects. For example: Secretarial Studies classes should have, or have access to, office equipment such as franking machine and telex.

My school education has helped me since I left school. You begin to understand fully certain things that you could just trip off the tongue. Everything has began to fall into place now.

I thought the courses in fifth year were very interesting, I enjoyed learning different things. In doing French & German you began to understand your English lessons better. Things seemed to all tie up.

I don't think the amount of time to you had to spend on work was about right. I myself could have done with an extra month to six weeks. Everything was crammed into such a short space of time.

In our school your prelims were before the Christmas holidays so you had to study, or to start to study, about two months in advance, but your course had hardly started and you weren't exactly sure as to what you should do.

Then, after Christmas it was straight into working for the actual exams. You did not seem to have any breathing space in between the two.

During exams in our school the teachers were very helpful you could go to see them and try to straighten out last minute problems. This way you personally were given more attention. I think if class numbers were decreased you would have a better chance in exams, because more time would be dedicated to say a class of fifteen than to a class of twenty-five. Teachers could devote time to a pupils' specific difficulty in a certain subject individually, rather than just explain it to the whole class in order that the pupil would grasp the problem, but this is not always the case. To finalise I think that all in all the teachers in our school were a tremendous help, the only hindrance in *my* opinion was the time factor.

*Female, Highers. Office junior.*

# 6.   Guidance and Careers

"More time could be spent with the
pupils explaining just how hard it is
to get a job"

"The subjects I took were ones that
I enjoyed not ones that I thought
would help me to get a job"

"I think the education should be
changed"

**Non-certificate leavers**


Yes I saw my guidance teacher. All I wanted to know about getting a job was mentiond in our (S.E) Social Education Class. They helped a lot by talking in that period at school. Other teachers weren't really helpful. I saw the Careers Officer once or twice and he gave me a list of some factories in my area to which I could write away to. He gave me the addresses of them which was very helpful. I got a job just before I left school and I started just after Christmas in January. So I was lucky.

> *Female, non-certificate. Packer in clothing factory.*



The guidance teacher was helpful, and so was the careers officer, they are very patient. they explain everything step by step, and they also help you, to find a job, explaining what to do when you get there, appearance etc.
I visited the careers officer every week for about two months, I found out something new every week. they didnt know much about the hotel trade, which I am interested in.
The teachers are helpful when in first, second, third year, I find they dont bother once you reach fourth year.

> *Female, non-certificate. Unemployed.*



I seen my guidance teacher but not very often and as for getting help from teachers it mainly seemed to be certain ones that got helped but I was'nt one.
I seen the careers officer about three times but that did'nt really help any. When I left school I tried for a job as an H.G.V. mechanic, I got an interview but the person that got it had someone speaking for him so I tried the pits and got in, its a really good pay for my age but I'd rather have been a mechanic. One thing I learned when I left school it's not what you know, it's who you know.

> *Male, non-certificate. On a mining apprenticeship. (Father a mining instructor.)*



The teachers & guidance teachers were very helpfull but I never went to school now
I regret it
I now am married have a baby boy and another one on it's way.

> *Female, non-certificate. Not looking for work.*

When (you are) in your fourth year and are planning to leave maybe teachers could give pupils some idea of what it is going to be like when they leave, how to face interviews, how to go about looking for a job, what kind of questions they might be asked etc., I saw a guidance teacher at school and because this lady was a stranger to me I found it very difficult to talk to her and to try to explain what I wanted to do when I left school so in the end I did not like seeing her and did not want help from her but preferred to see my own house mistress or master or maybe another teacher that I got on well with or found it easy to talk with.

I left school with no knowledge of any other things than what we got at school so when I left my mother helped me a lot telling me where to go for jobs (Job Centre) and where to look e.g. the newspapers. I started out with no experience in Secretarial but got a job as a Junior in a Layers Office and worked my way up from there doing filing, photo-copying, mail, deliveries and a little typing then went onto night school for typing and shorthand and I earned my self promotion two times within a year of working then left my first job to go to another firm and work as an Audio typist. I think if someone who does leave school just now without any certificates (I may add that they would be a lot better off staying on as I found out for myself employers are looking for young people with certificates of some kind and a good reference from school) if they are lucky enough to get a job, if they work hard and show that they want to learn and do something with themselves they will get on well enough and sometimes they are better off in a job than staying on at school and not enjoying it. I would advise any school leaver to stay on at school until they had a job and got as much experience in anything they can get rather than having to sign on the dole and hang around Job Centres and Employment Offices as this can get very depressing and turns a lot of people to not bothering at all.

*Female, non-certificate. Audio typist.*

**O grade leavers**

In my last year at school I still didn't know what I wanted to do when I left school, so I did look for help with guidence teachers and career officers. I wanted to know what kind of jobs I would be suitable for and what to expect. I was'nt really answered all that well, eg I did'nt know what to expect or what to do when going to the doll. I was well informed on interveiws and application forms etc. The subjects I took were ones that I enjoyed not ones that I thought would help me to get a job. I think subjects should not be chosen but that a more developed base on all subjects should be used ie as in 1st and 2nd years, because many people do not really know what they want to do in life after school.

*Male, O grades. Apprentice fitter/turner in shipbuilding industry.*


On the whole the teachers were most unhelpful and had the attitude of "it is your life i've got a job" so to speak. I never once saw my guidance teacher and was never once asked if I wanted to see her. The only communication I had with any teachers about leaving school was my English teacher who only made a big joke out of it.

I met the careers officer once for a session which lasted for about ten minutes at the most and all he told me was I should stay on and sit 'Highers'. that or either work in a bank.

The whole out-look to helping school-leavers get a job could be very much improved. More time could be spent with the pupils explaining just how hard it is to get a job and what kind of jobs they would be best suited to, and more careers people brought in to gife more professional and helpful advice.

*Female, O-grades. Office junior.*


We weren't told what it was going to be like when we left school. We should be told more on how to go about getting a job and how to cope with being unemployed and about courses and training schemes available to us. I think the education should be changed. When you get to third year I think you should be interviewed and discuss different careers. Then if someone wanted to be an engineer or a technician they would have third and fourth year to study and be trained in this field and when they leave school they will have learned the first year of engineering or whatever and employers will take on school leavers as they have been trained and will know what to do in a job.

When I left school I wasn't sure what I was supposed to do so I phoned a friend and she said she was going to the careers office so I went along with her and was given a card to come back for an interview. At my interview my careers officer discussed my subjects and asked me what career I wanted. I didn't know so I said clerical. He asked me if I would consider going back to school if I got good grades and take highers. He gave me a card to take to the unemployment bureau so I could sign on. When I went I didn't know what I was to do so I sat down and waited for someone to call me over. I have to fill in forms and was given another card and told to come back each week. When I got a phone call to go for my first interview I didn't know what I was to do or say at it as no one had ever discussed this with me.

*Female, O-grades. Clerical assistant.*

**Highers leavers**

Our guidance teacher, to me was of absolutely no use. In sixth year she only appeared every now and again to check attendance. There was nobody who would sit and actually *listen* to your hopes career-wise, and *advise* you. The careers officer was okay, as long as you entered her room with a definite career choice, and she could tell you what colleges or universities did the course. If you did not have a clue what to do, she seemed lost and its surprising the amount of girls she thought would make nurses! Considering I did not really know what profession to enter at the end of sixth year, I am glad that I took the H.N.D. Business Studies as I do find it interesting, and i feel it gives me a wide choice of jobs (if available). This is lucky considering I picked the course by leafing through the [] prospectus looking for a course that required '3' highers and 6 O grades!!

> *Female, 3 Highers and 6 O grades. Doing business studies at an FE college.*

I saw a Guidance teacher once a year, but as most of the time I had no problems these meetings were short. They did prove useful to others: but the one time I needed help – at the end of 4th year when I wanted to drop Latin and continue with History, she could not help. The Careers officer was of no real help – I chose my course at University by reading the prospectus myself – most of the other information I needed was readily available in the careers library. Many of my friends felt the same. However those of our friends who left after fourth and fifth and who were aiming to get a job straight from school got a lot more help and advice from the career's officers and found their appointments more useful, often making extra appointments. I saw a Careers officer once a year – in 4th, 5th and 6th year (perhaps also in 3rd).

> *Female, Highers. Studying languages at university.*

The careers officer wasn't very enthusiastic about prospects of going to art college.

A lot of the teachers, I felt, in my 5th year, weren't very interested in what I was going to do when I left.

The best thing about my school was, because I wanted to go to Art college, that the art department, the teachers couldn't have been more helpful. One more point I would like to make is that when I have been looking for any ordinary job, office, shop or factory, the fact that I have 'highers' has put them off employing me because I am *over qualified*.

*Female, Highers. Currently unemployed, applying to art college.*

# 7.  YOP and WEEP

"It is experience, and that's what a
lot of employers want"

                                              "Are they not an excuse for cheap
labour?"

"(It) might make them feel less
inhibited about being unemployed"

**Non-certificate leavers**

I think the YOP scheme is only cheap labour and the employers play on
it they have 1 for 6 mths then once the 6mths is up they get rid of them
and get another whereas probably if there was no YOP scheme they
would have to employ someone and give them a decent wage and they
would therefore get decent training. Depends on circumstances wether
or not they help them to get jobs. THEY ONLY SAVE YOU FROM
BEING LAZY!

> *Female, non-certificate. Joined a work experience scheme for one*
> *month, but now fully employed as a shop assistant.*

The schemes the government have provided for unemployment
teenagers seemed to be a good idea to begin with but now I'm not so sure.
In some cases they do provide experience, which will prove useful to
them in that type of job. later on. Employers are beginning to take
advantage of such schemes, if the employer has someone who is
unemployed on this scheme doing the same work as someone fully
employed why should he employ someone full-time when the
government is paying for the young person who can do the work just as
well as other full-time worker? Some people have been lucky and have
found a full time job at the end of the scheme but what about the ones
who have been on several schemes and have got nothing out of it at all.
They don't get paid enough for what they do – in other words its just
'slave labour'.

> *Male, non-certificate. On a work experience scheme as a canning*
> *assistant.*

There are not enough jobs not even on the youth opportunity training
scheme.
If the Government would stop cutting back on so many things to save
them money by closing down factorys that have hundreds of workers
there might not be so many unemployed.
I think the training scheme is good for young people but your only there
for six months and by the end of that you are fully trained for the job and
you have to start looking for something else.

> *Female, non-certificate. Sales assistant on a work experience*
> *scheme.*

I think the special scheme's for the unemployed are a very good idea, & I think that they do help a lot of the unemployed by giving them confidence and also experience which a lot of employers are looking for. I know that if I were out of a job & had been for sometime then I would definately try one of these schemes.

*Female, non-certificate. Telephonist/receptionist.*

## O grade leavers

I have only one comment to make. I am *16* years of age I myself work on a Y.O.P. scheme, I have worked there for about 8 months. I get paid £23.50 per week, for a *40* hour week. I get up at 7'oclock in time to get a lift at 8'oclock. As I live in [], which is about 32 *miles* from Edinburgh. I get a lift at 8'o'clock at [] to take me to [], which is 18 miles away, for 8.30am. I finish work at 4.30 to catch the bus to reach [] for 5.00pm. it costs me £12.95 per week for bus fairs, the government pay £8.95, but I pay the other £4.00. Thus leaving me with £19.50 per week, I think this is slave Labour for a 40 hour week. But I have now choice in the matter because I cannot get a job in my area I have to taravel for one, although it is just a Y.O.P. scheme. Plus when you get their they treat you as if your still at school, and I think they don't care anyway. I must admit they try to find jobs, but its useless if there is no jobs to find. PS *Excuse the handwriting but I am half asleep*

*Male, O grades. On a work experience scheme in woodwork.*

I thing goverment special schemes for unemployed young people is a good thing. It is experience, and that's what a lot of employers want. It also keeps young people from walking about the streets, and being on social security.

Yes, the special schemes do help to get young people jobs. A person who has been at college or on a special scheme has a very good chance to get a really good job. A much better chance than, they had when they left school. They also help people to be independant, tidy, ambitious, and more happy with life. I think you would see a big change in alot of young people who have been on the dole for months and finally gets a job.

*Female, O grades. On a secretarial course.*

Since leaving school I've only been able to find work on a scheme. I find the scheme good in some ways and bad in others. It was good for me because I've now been offered a full time job with the employer I'm with. It was bad at first because they tried to shrugg you off with bad jobs and did'nt bother taking time to teach you as they think you'll only be there for six months. I think the scheme in some cases could be used by employers as cheap labour and when your'e six months is up they get rid of you and get some body else on the same scheme.

*Male, O grades. Butcher, started as participant of a work experience scheme, and permanent job subsequently offered.*

**Highers leavers**

In principle, the Govt training schemes seem perfectly feesable but in reality are they not a superficial time filler which at least keeps the unemployed statistics down for a few weeks to staive off political aggro? Are they not an excuse for cheap labour? The jobs that are available on these schemes are for mostly manual work and the scope catered for is ridiculously small and insulting – after all whats the point of going to school in order to be hit with jobs as labourers in zoos and phoney stuff like that. I suppose they at least give an important insight into the working environment of the 'oldees' of society, the normals (a to z as Sheena Easton would say) people of the "proper" world.

*Male, Highers. Waiting to start a full-time course in journalism.*

I have experienced the government's special employment schemes at first hand and I think it is a scandalous use of unemployed youngsters, to do jobs no-one else wants to do, at a wage which is a joke. They just depress and they do not help because there is no point in working for 6 months and then moving to another as there is no opportunity to consolidate all the skills and knowledge learnt in this time and put them to good use.

*Male, Highers. On a government scheme as a trainee bank officer.*

I also think the governments special schemes for unemployed young people are good because they make people feel useful, wanted and occuppied. They can also prepare and train young people for a future career. It can also help them socially becuase they will meet other people, many like themselves and so might make them feel less inhibited about being unemployed.

*Female, Highers. Banking officer.*

# 8.   Unemployment – and Employment

"The things I found difficult about
finding a job is that there is no jobs
going for us"

"All I know is that I am bloody
grateful for a job that is interesting,
enjoyable and I love it"

"I'm just one of the 3 million"

**Non-certificate leavers**

I also object to having to travel 32 miles each way once a fortnight (when I'm unemployed) to the employment office in [] to be asked the same questions. Are you trying to find work, where have you tried & so on. This is a rural area & there are only so many places one can try. I've tried them all several times. Theres nothing to look to the future for.
*Male, non-certificate. Finishing a work experience scheme.*

I think that there should be more done for the unemployed school leaver. I suppose I am one of the lucky ones because I think the Guards are the Elite of the British Army. I enjoy the life although the training is difficult to start with. As far as helping youngsters look for jobs I would cut out married women working unless they really have to and I would bring the retiral age of women to 55yrs & men to 60 years. I do not know if my comments will be helpful but I hope they will be.
Yours faithfully
*Male, non-certificate. Guardsman in armed forces.*

People think because youre on the brew you never look for work but I would personally like to be working than sitting about all day and achieving nothing.
*Female, non-certificate. Unemployed.*

The things I found difficult about finding a job is that there is no jobs going for us, The only jobs that are going are one's for people with O'grade's and highers, or 16 year olds, 18 year olds and over 21s. Being seventeen is a very difficult age to be at to get a job.
*Female, non-certificate. Unemployed.*

**O grade leavers**

My attitude was I would be as well getting out of school as soon as I could and find a job since they are getting harder to come by as the days go on. Also I feel qualifications are not as important anymore, if you can prove to someone you are a good, efficient worker, you can pick things up quickly, dress properly, speak nicely, answer telephones correctly & have a good temperament with customers. It isn't so difficult to find a job.

I left school at 15, after my o'levels, gave my self a bit of a break before putting my mind down to work. I enrolled at [] technical college, for French higher & shorthand.

I had an evening class for French and spent a day once a week for shorthand/typing. I enjoyed college as I did school, but I was just doing this to learn more about what I wanted.

I enjoy meeting people. I feel I'm a very sociable person, and my parents had suggested being a receptionist, and by chance my father has a few friends who are big in Travel Agency, or Tour Operators business. He arranged for me to talk to someone in this line and it sounded interesting. So in August just as I was beginning to feel bored, I had another person who was willing to talk to me in []. I went into [], just wore a skirt shirt & jacket made my self look presentable. I spoke to the person and wasn't successful, but I didn't give up because I had been put down. I wandered about [] and went into every travel or tour company I came across. Tired and beginning to give up with all the polite 'nos', I had on my way to going home I spotted another place, so I thought I'd go in, I was introduced to one of the directors of the firm, there wasn't a vacancy in the travel department, but there may be a vacancy for the shipping side soon, so I left feeling pleased with my efforts. We kept in touch and it so happened a vacancy came up in [] in the Travel Department and I was asked to go for an interview over the phone and later received a letter saying what day I could start.

If you give a good impression, and ask the right questions, its easy. What impressed the was that I had done it all off my own back. Having been well brought up and having a good education makes all the difference as it shows. But the qualifications were not important. I hope this will be of some help in your survey and that the last two pages have been of some interest. Thank you.

*PS.* I had to stop college as we are not given the opportunity of day-release. And with starting work & learning a lot I was feeling I couldn't cope with an evening class either.

*Female, O grades. Copy typist with a travel agency.*


I think the young people should get together and raise enough money to rebuild old warehouses etc and open them up some as hotels where you get catering, Secreterial, porters and all different kinds of jobs where they can train.

*Female, O grades. Time-keeper with a civil engineering company.*

I waited months for a Job and the only way I got one was through my boyfriends father who is, an Engineering deseigner. Besides that I dont think I would have got one. Nowadays you have to know Someone in a firm to get a job.

*Female, O grades. Machinist.*

### Highers leavers

I was only on the dole for approx. 3 months this time last year, but not being able to obtain a job makes one extremely apathetic to life, with an very depressing outlook on the rest of humanity.

*Female, Highers. Clerkess in an insurance company.*

It is difficult to say what should be done to help young people find jobs. I realise it must be the worst experience to wake up day after day knowing you have to go into the job centre yet again, then running out of bus fares to get there because your not earning the money to pay for them. I know it's easier said than done but the secret is never to give up hope.
All I know is that I am bloody grateful for a job that is interesting, enjoyable and I love it.

*Female, Highers. Trainee travel agent.*

I am disabled, and some of the difficulties that I have had in finding a job are, lack of facilities for disabled people in many factories and offices, lack of intrest by some of the employers, and disabled people not being considered for jobs and job schemes which are quite within their capabilities.

*Male, Highers. On a work experience scheme.*

I had two interviews followed by two starting dates from different banks-I had a choice.

*Female, Highers. Bank clerkess.*

Unfortunately, I cannot offer any alternatives to solve the unemployment problem. But, I'm no Polititian or Economist collecting a nice fat wage packet to inspire any words of wisdom. No, I'm just one of the 3 million.

*Male, Highers. Unemployed.*

## 9. Further Education

"I hope the course will help me find
some kind of job"

"During the course I felt it very
difficult to make ends meet"

"At College you where treated like
an adult for it was up to yourself if
you wanted to go or not, for it was
for your own benefit"

**Non-certificate leavers**

School helped me in a way to go to college, for I wanted to learn more, for I felt I had'nt learned enough education to go out straight into work. At college I took a Junior Secretarial Course, which I had never taken typing or anything like this before. I sat exams at the end of the year and got all the certificates which helped me in finding a job. At College you where treated like an adult for it was up to yourself if you wanted to go or not, for it was for your own benefit.

*Female, non-certificate. Clerical worker.*

So I really don't think improving (school) is what is needed apart from the fact that I don't think they encourage you for college or any other further education which I think is a waste because I am now like alot of people unemployed altogether since I left school in 1979 eleven months in all and having only one youth opportunity scheme so if I had went on to college I could have trained for a better job and studied for qualifications which would help me find a job faster than I have already experienced. I think teachers should encourage pupils more now than ever before and point out all the advantages which would be acheived at college rather than leaving school like thousands of school pupils and signing on once a fortnight and getting out a couple of nights, and you always get the people who slag us for being so called "Scroungers".

*Female, non-certificate. Unemployed.*

After I left the school I went on a short training course at []. Then I went on a government scheme to [] where I worked for about three months then I started full time. No-one has ever tried to encourage me to go to college although I had thought about going to night school to take a Secretarial Course but I didn't know how to go about it.

*Female, non-certificate. Warehouse worker.*

About three months ago my friend and I were thinking about going to night school, and then sitting our 'O' levels. We wanted to emigrate to Australia and stay, and we thought we would have a better chance of getting a good job with some 'O' levels. Because its not going to be very good spending the rest of your life working at something you don't like doing, or won't pay any attention to, or learn anything from.

*Female, non-certificate. Dish washer.*

**O grade leavers**

I spent 2 years studying for my English 'O' level and never got it, but at college I was only there for about 4 or 5 months and then sat my junior SCOTBEC English and passed it and am now sitting SCOTBEC English this month. So I would say my English teacher at college is better than the one from school and also easier to understand. My school told me about college and so I decided I would leave school and go to college. I have found shorthand quite difficult but after a time you get to understand it.

*Female, O grades. Doing a secretarial course at an FE college.*

College has been good it's taugh me how to get on better with adults, because the teachers treat you like an adult and you can talk openly about your personal problems and feelings. The course has also taught me useful things pertaining to the course. Going to college has also helped me grow up and be a bit more independent and make me think and do for myself. I will miss College when I leave in May more than I miss School. I hope the course will help me find some kind of job.

*Female, O grades. Doing a hotel receptionist course at an FE college.*

I am now at college and will be finished in a few months time During the course I felt it very difficult to make ends meet because I was not allowed a grant and my parents cannot afford to give me any money. I had to pay for my bus fares out of the money I earned in my Saturday job which was not a lot & my social life is non-existent because of the lack of money.

*Female, O grades. Doing a secretarial course at an FE college.*

**Highers leavers**

I am employed as a Banking Officer and part of my training, if desired by myself is to take exams set by the Institute of Bankers in Scotland. Towards this end [] College run a course catering for this syllabus, which I attend receiving Day Release from my employers. Why, when I subsidise full time University & College Students through tax do I have to pay for my own course, receive no grant and have to pay for my own

books. Financial help in even one of these areas would probably be a more just and equitable deal.
*Male, Highers. Trainee manager.*

I am now studying Social Science at []. It is not what I wanted but now that I am here I like it very much. It doesn't give me the chance to write (creatively) but it has made me more understanding of the society in which I live. I have friends at University & I'm glad now that I didn't go because they find it too formal & come home feeling deprived because they haven't got two toilets in their house. I am happy in what I'm doing but I realise how lucky I am.
*Male, Highers. Studying social science at an FE college.*

Since leaving school I started a college course and have been very disappointed. I received no grant although at the time I applied I was living on my own. The college treated us as children and were very strict about time keeping and attendance. To make sure no tuancy occured a censor card was issued and followed us through each class.
*Female, Highers. On a data processing course at an FE college.*

# 10.   University

"surely schools are there to give
knowledge and prepare the child for
adult hood and its final assault on
the world, not as a prelimenary
awakening for would-be graduates"

"It has however, taught me to
analyse & question much more
about life"

"To hell with all those Highers it's
the person who makes the teacher
not the stupid certificates on top of
the wardrobe"

At university I found myself lacking in knowledge of politics & economics, unable to communicate & make adult discussion. I think social skills should be emphasised at school & could be done quite easily in every classroom, by having tutorials where the subject being studied is discussed between teachers & a few pupils.
*Female, Highers. Studying nursing at university.*

To begin with I would like to say that I have found filling in this questionnaire very interesting and thought-provoking and hope that my opinions may prove helpful.

My first point is a very simple one. A school is only as good as the people in it and the relationship which exists between them. Good teachers are essential for success, both academically and in less tangible forms. I have found this to be the main difference between school and university. At university there is no feeling of group solidarity, such as existed in a class or year at school. Strangers meet for an hour then disperse and tend to remain in cliques. The student-lecturer relationship is much more formal and businesslike than in school. Even tutorials fail in this respect. I particularly miss this, as I am naturally rather introverted and need other people to bring me out.
*Male, Highers. Studying history at university.*

University is very enjoyable except for the impersonality of the tuition methods. It has however, taught me to analyse and question much more about life and also to be much more aware about current world affairs.
*Female, Highers. Studying for an arts degree at university.*

Only encouragement to go to University was being taken to Glasgow & Strathclyde University's open day. As far as the school was concerned those were the only 2 which existed. Pupils could have been given more encouragement. I found I had to find out an awful lot for myself especially with regards to [] University. I was discouraged to go to this one. Also discouraged to go to University after 5th year. School prefers you to stay on and do CSYS. I didn't stay for 6th year and although I find it difficult I don't find it any harder than some who stayed on for 6th year. I find University very enjoyable both accademically and socially, whereas school was annoying. Always one group of pupils who were the 'creme de la creme' and they were expected to go to university, all the others got very little encouragement.

Discouraged from taking 5 highers *and* one O grade Headmaster wanted me to do 4 highers & O grade. If I had done so I wouldn't have got into University because Sec Studies doesn't count as an entrance requirement. (We were not made aware of this fact until we started applying for University etc.)

*Female, Highers. Studying languages and education at university.*

I am now studying a very enjoyable course at [] University. I study my course, because I am interested in History and I think a diploma in Education will be useful. I'm conscious of the present job situation, but do not believe in studying a job orientated course unless I find it interesting. I enjoyed my school life very much. In sixth year I had a very good relationship with my teachers which extended to having a social drink with a few of them. My only regret at school was that after doing very well in my O'grades I did poorly in 5th and 6th year. I felt very reactionary against the exam system. Now I'm at University and working to try and qualify for an honours course. It is sad that so much emphasis is put on exams. The result is school courses (except CSYS) are very regular and boring. I also believe that if you have a grasp of exam technique half the battle is won. Many people do badly in exams and are intelligent, just a mediocre pupils attain good results.

I have no complaints about my school except that they should encourage more people to stay at school and try to qualify for university, but this is a universal problem.

*Male, Highers. Studying for a degree in education at university.*

At school we were obviously geared towards university and college, this in my opinion had an adverse effect on the insentives of many of the pupils. By this I mean, that some of the pupils who were put into lower classes/ non-certificate classes were, given much less attention than those of us who had "made the grade" so to speak. This is not the attitude necessary in a teaching institution, surely schools are there to give knowledge and prepare the child for adult hood and its final assault on the world, not as a preliminary awakening for would-be graduates.

*Female, Highers. Studying nursing at college.*

The school did not adequately prepare me for the type of study I would meet at University with the result that unless I work hard for resits over the summer I will be chucked out. I'm actually trying to think up a scheme to get me out of university without being thrown out like a dunce, because drop-outs tend to get the evil-eye from employers etc. Plus the fact that I got about five pence as a grant while everyone else gets thousands, I really don't know how they expect to attract electronics students with such a mean handout because the price of electronic gear is so steep these days. If things get any worse I'll have to take the guitar into [] Street and beg for money like an old tramp. I know this sounds very materialistic, but when my last instalment was £200 and a friend got £600, with which he bought a new cassette deck, a rifle and a drumkit as well as living in high style all term, it makes me wonder if its worth the effort of university. I've worked quite hard, and yet now I am penniless (completely) and I have to scrape up £50 for resits, while all my friends who did not go to University have cars and good jobs etc, and if I fail just one resit I'm chucked out.

*Male, Highers. Studying electronics at university.*

The school was very good on the purly accademic side. It developed an atmosphere inducive to study and the staff did all they could to help each individual pupil in their studies.
On the subject of Universities the school attempted to encourage all possible candidates to try.
The situation on sixth year was rather complicated by the fact that the school was fee paying. This meant it was important to have a large number of pupils in sixth year for the financial stability of the school especialy with the government stratergies on direct grant schools in the past few years. As far as pupils were concerned this meant that the merits of sixth year were *over* stressed and a fair view was not available to asses the merits in an individual case, properly. This accounts for the larger sixth year at the school than would be expected.
I have found after leaving at the end of fith year that I can cope amply with University and will probbably be qualified for a post a year earlier and thus have a better opertunity to get the job I want or to have an extra year at university or a short service comission in the armed forces before starting a job which I would be far less inclined to do had I spent the extra year at school.

*Male, Highers. Studying electronics at university.*

On the whole, the help the teachers gave to help get you through the exams was very good. The school was very University "biased" with all bright pupils being potential university students. Because of this I was encouraged (forced) to take subjects like french, instead of the subjects I was really interested in eg technical drawing, engineering science ect.

*Male, Highers. Studying data processing at an FE college.*


I went to a typical, very catholic like school which as well as encouraging girls to get good jobs also forced down the idea that we must foremostly be prepared to sacrafice ourselves to motherhood and being wives (a bore). I hated school, it is so far removed from the real world. But I cannot regret anything I learned even in a subject like Statistics which is absolutely no good to me now. My old school did try to get anyone with even a little talent to work hard and get to University. (But it's the same old boring subjects and places of learning). Nothing about Printing, Textiles, Modelling, Photography, Dancing (I missed my chance at art school due to this) University is a new world from school. I think people are better to go when a little older. Say 20 or 22. But I just want to get it over with. I want to teach little kids. Use my art, my imagination and by lively personality. To hell with all those Highers it's the person who makes the teacher not the stupid certificates on top of the wardrobe.

*Female, Highers. Studying for an arts degree at university.*

# Part II. A Cross-Section of Comments

"I Dont really know where to start here you know its like having an operation and sombody asking afterwards if it was sore or not Im glad you left this space yes i think you should read this part "very carfully" Because its only now that what really happens in the modern day school is coming clear to me"

I     **Non-certificate leavers**

1.    *Male, non-certificate. On a YOP scheme. Cleaner in District Council.*
      The only good thing about school, was when the school bell went, to let you know it was time to go home. The school would have been better if all the holigans got exspelled

2.    *Male, non-certificate. Hairdresser.*
      I do not think everything should be based on a final exam (O'levels) before you leave school. I think a written account of everything you have done since primary school would be a much better idea. I think this would put much less presure on pupils than O'levels do. I also think employers would find this much more helpfull.
      I think pupils should be treated with more respect. Teachers should definately not take their own problems out on pupils. The belt should also be withdrawn and replaced with something more suitable eg detension, lines and suspension.
      In my old school there were to maths teachers, one Indian and one Pakistani one of them (the pakistani) couldd not speak much English and could hardly read any, the other could not controll his pupils and he also walked around without any shoes on. Surely this cannot be allowed to continue.
      I think pupils should have more say in how schools are run, Student Unions are a great idea and their should be one in every school There should be more time spent on prepairing pupils for life when they leave and especially on politics.

3.    *Female, non-certificate. Overlocker in clothes factory.*
      My last year at school was not really worth it, when it came round to January to May. Most people tended just to stay at home because there was nothing worth going to school for.
      I have been working ever since I left school, I don't like the job very much but I wouldn't like to be on the dole.
      The education I received at school does not help me in the job I am in, but it would if I could get the job I wanted to do.
      The few months at school is boreing and you and friends just a carry on in class and most get into trouble nearer the leaving date.

4.  *Female, non-certificate. Unemployed.*
    I am 16 nearly 17 and out of work. I have never worked since I left
    school last year. I have been on one Y.O.P. scheme from
    September 1980 till March 1981 and I am know on Supplementary
    Benefit.
    At school I took one O'level Secretarial Studies. I also took the
    prelim in Food + Nutrition and Arithmetic but dropped these.
    My school education has not helped me because I always got
    nervous before the exams and couldn't concentrate. I think they
    should stop exams because you get to worked up before them.
    their was nothing really bad about the high school but they could
    of made it more enjoyable, some of the other schools in [] get a
    period too themselves to do what they want.

5.  *Male, non-certificate. Apprentice motor mechanic.*
    The ficillities for teenagers in this area are very bad. And also
    because of the unemployment teenagers have not enough money,
    and the boys that have not got a job are losing the head and are
    starting to steal anything they can for money and, also the
    Government are complaining about the crime rate, I predict the
    crime rate will double easily by next year and the cause is mainly
    by *unemployment* and I think you should also include this question
    in your next survey and you will probilly get the same answer as
    mine.

6.  *Female, non-certificate. Employed in food trade.*
    I'AM 16 YRS OLD I'M SMALL FOR MY AGE I HAVE FOUR
    SISTERS & THREE BROTHERS MY MOTHER DOSE NOT
    WORK BY FATHER HAS WORKED IN AFRICIA FOR THE
    PAST 4 YEARS. I ALSO HAVE 5 NIECE'S & 3 NEPHEW'S. I
    HAVE A RESPECTABLE HOME AND I HAVE MANY
    FRIEND'S I HAVE JUST STARTED A JOB IN [].
    THE THINGS THAT WERE GOOD ABOUT MY SCHOOL
    WERE THAT WE HAD SO MANY SUBJECT'S TO CHOOSE
    FROM AND DIFFRENT TEACHERS SO YOU DIDN'T
    REALLY GET FED UP WITH THE SAME ONE ALL THE
    TIME SO YOU CAN ENJOY YOUR SUBJECTS.
    MY LIFE SINCE LEAVING SCHOOL HAS BEEN GOOD SO
    FAR I HAVE HAD A JOB CAREAS FOR 6 MONTH'S WHICH
    I THINK IS M ONE BIT UNESSARY SCANDEL WHICH I DO

NOT APROVE OF. BUT SINCE THAT I HAVE GOT A FULL
TIME JOB FOR A WHILE.
MY SCHOOL EDUCATION HAS NOT HELPED ME AS I DO
NOT NEED ANY CERTIAN GRADES FOR THE SORT OF
JOB THAT I ENJOY DOING AND WHAT I LIKE TO DO.
NOTHING THAT I CAN REMEMBER HAPPENED AT
SCHOOL BECAUSE I WAS NOT THEIR VERY OFTEN. BUT
AFTER SCHOOL A LOT OF GOOD & BAD THING'S HAVE
HAPPENED WITH FRIEND'S & FAMILIES WHAT I DON'T
CARE TO REMEMBER A THING I NEVER DONE AT
SCHOOL WAS GOING SWIMMING AND ALSO GO TO
DISCO'S BUT NOW I DO AND LEAVING SCHOOL WAS
THE BEST THING OF MY LIFE (SO FAR).


7.   *Female, non-certificate. Works in office.*
When I attended [], I found I had alot more friends than I have now.
At school I sat a City & Guilds exam. This was under Commercial
Studies. The exams I took for this were - Modern Studies ,
Arithmetic, Secretarial Studies, Social Economics This was good
because if you weren't good enough to pass o' levels this Course
helped you to get some qualification before leaving school
At the end of May I passed this exam and received a certificate for
it. The schoolteachers told us this was just like an o'level, but I have
found when I started work, theses bosses don't seem to except it,
they say i've no qualfications, and have no chance of finding a
proper job.
Also since Ive left school ive been on three of these "YOP" courses
two I stuck and the other i didn't, but Ive found that you can't get
off them was your on them, the money is terrible, when you think
of it, you are working a full week doing the same job as other people
and finding they are earning twice as much as you, and at the end
of it you can't even afford to go out or buy food once you've handed
in your House keeping Money and paid bus fares etc.
I would like to see more young folk get proper jobs, because at the
end of these six months training courses you find that some of these
bosses have no intention of keeping you on.
Since leaving school my life has become worse. Though I think my
education has helped me alittle Sometimes Ive wished I had stayed
on at schol and took more exams that may have helped me find a
better job, though I don't think that counts anymore.
Also I have'nt as many friends as I used too have.

8.  *Female, non-certificate. Junior secretarial course at college.*
    At the moment I am attending [] on a full time Junior Secretarial course which started in August 1980 and finishes in June 1981. I am going to be taking four Scotbec exams, English, typing, office practice and shorthand and then I hope to get a office Job. I think that by going to the college for further Education has helped me very much, I have learned more Secretarial and Office work at college more than what I did when I was at school, the teachers were very good and helpfull and I have made many new friends.
    The thing that was good about my school was the teachers helped me as much as they could, I also had many friends at school. The thing that could have been made better is more authority over the Pupils by making it compulsary to wear their uniform, because it would have made the school much nicer.
    My life since leaving school has been better I feel that I have more responsibility, and make decisions myself.
    Yes my school Education has helped me it has prepared me for the outside world.

9.  *Female, non-certificate. On a YOP scheme in a youth centre.*
    When I was in fourth year I didn't realise how important good grades were. I did study for my exams although it didn't do me any good. Some of the teachers didn't want to know you're problems they only wanted to know how the clever ones were finding the work. I did complain to my house mistress but no action was taken. I think even if I had got my O' levels it wouldn't have helped me any as I want to go into hairdressing and no qualifications are needed.
    I am now on a Youth Opportunity Programme and I quite enjoy it although I have no hope in my opinion of being kept on.
    The scheme lasts for a year although I am hoping to leave in August to go into hairdressing college. If I could get a full time job in a shop or cafe I would take it as I've worked part time in a cafe as a waitress and I thought it was great.
    The scheme I'm on gives a lot of help in preparation to finding full time work such as letter writing and how to arrive at an interview. The scheme is very good.

10. *Female, non-certificate. Unemployed.*
    School was quite good but did not Like some of the teachers. The teachers only had time for pupils that were sitting o'levels and I did

not sit any o'levels. My education did not help me get a job which I have been looking for the past year. I have only been on a six month course and getting payed23.50 for doing full time work the same as the rest in the shop was doing. When I left school I had no hope of getting a job so I tryed the course and found it was good but not a lot of money for the work that I did.


11. *Male, non-certificate. Unemployed.*
I Dont really know where to start here you know its like having an operation and sombody asking afterwards if it was sore or not Im glad you left this space yes i think you should read this part "very carfully" Because its only now that what really happens in the modern day school is coming clear to me.

Okay Education is a good thing but you want to know what they taught me Yes I think I should tell you it starts early when kids not up to academic standard a particulr *Academic* standard are placed in whats comonly known as the *Daft* group where they learn Humileation a very cold lonly Humileation I know Because I was in a group yes the Daft group I was the one to survive whats called Primary Education mabe because I realized in time what the Daft group was Designed for I only realized because as I wached the kids around me clam up and by allowing themselves to become so inferior they became just to afraid to open up the rest of there school lives would be spent in the Daft group Yes thats right there all in factories now just doing what there told to bloody scared to Do anything else they were sensetive feeling children once now there nothing more than zombies or slaves take your pick

you ask was the last year worthwhile I said no by that time the Damage had already been Done

humileation and fear thats what I learned at primary then I learned how to Hate and then how to fight back very soon I was at war with the whole System I knew I could never beat the System but I had to fight if only to hang on to my own Sensetivity and the right to be me and not what it wanted me to be I Disrupted the teacher not the class and by Playing them at thier own game I soom became notorias I would have to be stamped out before this Deasease of individuality couht on regretfuly it never Did to my friends I was nothing more than a guy who somehow Drove all the teachers mad I think some reconised what I was going on but were to brain washed and scared to help then one Day there Didn't Seam much point any more the long fight was ended I knew it and so Did the top teachers I was expelled the Same Day but as in a war of any shape or size

THERE CAN BE NO WINNERS
but the Fight goes on
Good luck

12.    *Female, non-certificate. Unemployed.*
       Nothing was good about my school the teachers could have been
       more understanding and helpfull. My life has been a bore trying to
       find Jobs, No School education hasnt helped me because I was
       hardly ever there but now I wish I had stuck into school.

13.    *Female, non-certificate. Kitchen assistant.*
       Dr Garner,
       The school I went to some teachers tried to prepare us for our life
       after school but some did not, I do not regret leaving school early
       but sometimes wonder if It would have helped me get a job sooner
       I had been looking for a job for *Two months*, when my brother's
       friend said they needed more staff at the restaurant I applied for the
       job and have been there ever since. I am thankful for the fact that
       I have a job but I can also say my schooling didn't seem to come
       into any use at my interview it was just manners and respectability
       that helps in a job like mine
       Yours sincerely

14.    *Female, non-certificate. Nursery nurse.*
       School Could be made better if everyone got to siT "O" levels.
       Since leaving school I cannot find a Job. School education has
       helped me to get on some Courses but not much. At school I went
       on a work experience course in the [] (Resturant) but did not help
       me afterwards. but I do voluntry work in the local Community
       Centre. And this has helped Quite a lot.

15.    *Female, non-certificate. Box maker.*
       When I stared school I was a quit shy child. And I was Just lift to
       sit all thought shcool if you quit and shy you just get to sit. I started
       hight school. I enjoyed cooking but not sewing as the teacher all
       ways picked on me she had to her pets in the class and if she did
       not like you she made youer life hell. I allso liked child care that
       was going out of school to look after children in an nursery school.
       I fell if I had lern more in school. I would have enjoyed school more.
       I have now stared work. I have been working for 1 1/2 years. When
       starting work I thought it would be the same as school but it was
       differnt. I had to lern things that you are showen quickly. I fell I
       lernt a lot more since I started work than I ever lernt at school. At
       work ever one mixes and you not left. I enjoy working.

16.   *Female, non-certificate. Working in wool mill.*
      My name is []. I am 5ft 5in with brown hair, & blue eyes. I work
      at []. I like working in [] there are a lot of interesting things about
      the mill, I was suppose to, be a invisable mending, I was to slow to
      make up my performance, so I got put on the Burling. I have a lot
      of friend in my work there are some old people and young too. I
      work 40 hours a week it much longer than school. When I was at
      school I enjoyed all my subjects, cooking was my best Subject. The
      teachers was very kind and I was very kind to them. My education
      did help me. Teachers could be more strickter what they are, and
      paid more attention on their job. Leaving School was horriable
      because I have lost all my friends I just see some of my friends now
      and again I went out more times than I did at school. I going out
      with [] he is the same age as me.
      PS why are you asking about my mother and father.

17.   *Female, non-certificate. Christmas leaver. On an office training
      course.*
      I left school at Christmas 79'. I have had a full time job and the rest
      have been YOP. I am on a 12 week training course with [] at the
      present. when I first left school I hated it cause there was no jobs,
      since then it seems to have got worse.
      I wish I had stayed on at school and took my O'levels. I liked school
      cause all my friends were there.

18.   *Female, non-certificate. Sales person.*
      At the moment I work in a food shop I don't like it very much. At
      my school there is to many hoolagens. My headmaster did'nt help
      much Because everyone wanted to get back as him because he
      treated you like dirt My teachers did'nt care about as long as you
      came to School. My School could be better if teacher gave pupils
      time and care and tryed to understand your problems.

19.   *Female, non-certificate. Office junior.*
      When I left school in May 1980 I was unemployed till September
      then I went to College for 3 months the started in YOP in [] Housing
      Association till May then I started a job which I got before i was
      to leave the YOP. And that is the job I am in just now. []
      School was no good to me well so I think.
      Sorry I could'nt write back before as I was bissey with my
      interviews.

20.    *Female, non-certificate. Unemployed.*
At the school I went to I did not leave until fifth year because i was to young. to leave in the fourth year.
What would make the school better would be if the teachers paid more attention to the less intelligent one's than paying all attention to all the bright kids. who sit o levels and A levels. for at school it was worth while if you got some education because when you leave it doe's help when looking for work. but since I have left school I have had one job and I never got it throw my careers officer it was throw my sister because I think you have a better chance of getting a job if you know someone who works where you look for a job.
After I left school I regesterd at my careers office they sent me for two interveiws since then they have never sent for me again. because there are more people in unemployment now than ever. When I went to school I didn't really think about looking for a job because I didn't really think about work as I really didn't know what it would be like out side of schools. I think this would be a good thing to be disgussed more at school and at home.

21.    *Male, non-certificate. On a YOP scheme in a butcher's shop.*
The things that were good about school was meeting people and making friends or if you got a teacher you could talk to in your own way and he or she would listen.
What could be made better?: The way some of the teachers treat you and I think there should be a wider range of subjects to pick from. One thing I think the school should do is have a class for what is going to happen to you when you leave school and explain how you are going to fill in forms eg applications forms supplementary benifit forms etc. And how you would go about interviews for jobs. My life has been so,so since I left school I got a yop scheme at a brickwork and that was hard work and it was quite a distance away from where I live so it cost me quite a bit for bus fares and by time I paid my ways I had hardly any money left. I am now working on another yop scheme in a butchers but when my time is up (6 months) I have to get the chance to become a butcher, because I have got an apprenticeship out of it.
Has you school education helped you? some of my school education has helped me eg Arithmetic for counting, food and Nutrition couses for food uses whats good for you and what is not. English how to use a word when speaking to someone, and how to speak correctly.
The things that happened at school: well quite a few of us used to get belted for smoking. We would play football round outside the

pE department becaus the pE Teacher would rather we played rugby and we would play there just to spite him. We used to sneak into the dinner hall before it was our time so we could go to the shops at dinner time. Some of the teachers would walk around the grounds of the school and carry on with some of the pupils.

22.    *Female, non-certificate. Unemployed.*

Well the thing's I found good about my school were the wide range of sporting facilitie's also the way the teacher's tried there best to help us when we had a problem with our work or teacher's. Well at first I was sorry I left school in the first place as it was borring sitting in the house and I missed my friend's and of course I couldn't find a job. I went into all the shop's in the next town from me, asking about job's but of course never got one.

I was interested in swimming so I met my friend's at the swimming pool every Tuesday and Thursday night.

What I think could be made better is the History. What I mean is I think they should have learned us more about the future and less about the History or they should have had a subject about the future as well as the History as some people like to learn something about the future as well as History. Yes my school education has helped me in alot of way's like how to make friend's and how to read + write ect. And it help me to do the write thing which was to be write and thing's which were in the wrong.

Well at school when I fell out anyone they used to say things behind my back and of course it got carried back to me and I would have pulled her up about it then it would end up as a fight and of course I was the one who would get into trouble about it from my house master whom I did'nt really like as when one of my friend's got into trouble my house master brought me into it and it had nothing to do with me and I would be in trouble again.

After school I used to go out my friend's and hang about [] cross but now that I have left school I go to parties + disco's and get to know more folk and get date's with many boy's and run about with different girls but the problem is that all my friend's which have left school has job's except me and I have tried my best but can't find a job any where at all.

Well to be quiet honest with you I go to [] disco's as well, it is a home for boy's but they're quiet good and the boy's are very nice to get on with and very nice to got out with. Our girls can talk to the [] boy's better than we can talk to our boy's, as we dont realy like them as they are undesent and unpliot to girl's.

23.    *Male, non-certificate. Unemployed.*
       *I am fed* up because I am out of work. And try every day to try and
       get a job to no availl.

24.    *Male, non-certificate. On a construction course.*
       The first two years of school life for me were hell. Third year
       gradually got to grips with me, then fourth year the best year of
       school for me. Then once I left school I went on the dole and the
       depression and boredom started. Being unemployed was terrible,
       But being employed wasnt so good as I thought my first job was as
       a labourer on a golf course sight and it was hellish I *worked* and
       *worked* and because I was the only boy thier who came from a
       certain town I was subject to terrible beatings. After that I got a job
       with my local burgh, in the cleansing dept. with the youth
       opportunities scheme 23.50 a week....as far as I was concerned it
       was'nt called experience it was called exploytation and it was £23.50
       for doing a man's work full time worker coming out with three times
       the amount. The employer's for everyone (every yop) in the
       country are getting cheap labour, not even cheap labour. labour
       they dont pay anybody a penny for, and they expect us yops to pitch
       in like right MUGS. Im not afraid of work especially for, a descent
       wage and a descent atmosphere toward's the work. and Im sure
       every yop in thier right mind think the same. Thankyou.

25.    *Male, non-certificate. Medical clerk in hospital.*
       I would have liked the teachers at school to put off more time to
       help pupils like myself who weren't so clever to do better. The
       teachers were more interested in the clever ones and the not so
       clever were forgotten about. I was taught in Primary School with
       coloured rods and it was only in late school life that it was
       discovered I was coloured blind, and if I had been taught at the
       beginning by another method perhaps I might have done better at
       Maths etc.
       It is very disappointing at the end of 6 months that you don't get
       a chance to a full time job when you are with a YOP scheme. A boy
       is being interviewed for your job a week before you finish. This
       seems very unfair that employers can get new boys and girls so easily
       with a YOP scheme rather than train and give a person a chance
       to prove oneself in a permanent job. It is very disappointing for
       young boys and girls leaving school at the moment to have no choice
       of jobs and very dishearting.

26. *Female, non-certificate. Christmas leaver. Unemployed.*
In my fourth year I was determined nothing was going to stop my leaving in the December lot. You see I was a year older than some in my year so I was 16 in November, I left in December, and I should have sat my 4 O Grades in the following May.
My parents cokeds me but I was so determined I was going to leave.
I have never been happier since I left. I am unemployed at the moment, since January in fact, but I have applied for many jobs which some people dont even have the courtesy to reply too.
My favourite subject from the beginning of school was english. I had [] from 1st year and we became very good friends. I had him up until 3rd year, the year I was to study for my O Grade. Then I went into 4th year I was placed with another teacher. This just set me back completely. She done her teaching completely different from him and so I feel I would have failed my English O Grade anyway. And for his sake I just wanted to pass, because when picking my subjects I was refused English, but he fought for me and I got it. Then my friends and I started an 'Anti Abortion Group' he helped us through with it all and was always there for us to talk to.
He left just after I did, in the January. We still keep in good contact although he stays in []
So you see my 4th year was hell.

27. *Male, non-certificate. Unemployed.*
Nothing to tell as all I do is Look for jobs and When I was at school I didn't like it and never went very mutch.

28. *Female, non-certificate. General shop assistant.*
I am 17 years old and have been left school for nearly a year now. I work in shop which to not like all that much. But I still am looking for a better job. But I do not think I will get one because I did'nt get my O Grades. I tried my best and I did'nt get them . Well there is one reason why I did'nt get them and I would put down to the school. Because in English their was half the class was doing O Grade and the rest were not. and people who were not doing O Grade just sat and spoke and just fooled around and the other people who were trying to do work did'nt get Peace and queit they needed. This was the same in my Arithmatic class.
But in all my other class it was great. I went to [] which is a new school with great working conditions. And the best equipment that any young People going to the secondary school could want for a

better education. I would advise to take advantage of this if the want a good job. Because I have experienced being left with a job I do not like. Throw do have a good Education. But I would tell people to stick in and do well. But I remember before I left school I wrote away to company in apply for a Job and 3/4 of them did not reply. And when I replyed and asked you along for a interview and at the end of the interview the told you that the want some with more Experience. Well to me young people will not get the Experience if company's are not willing to take them on So some are left to go to collage and Some stay on at school. But I feel Sorry for those who I have never had the chance to sit O Grades. Because they will find it hard to get and job and when they to do get a job they get and thats why we get the troubler makers all because some company are not willing to give not peopll a chance.

**II    O grade leavers**

29.    *Female, O grades. Christmas leaver. Chemist sales assistant.*
After fourth year, instead of being able to leave at the summer
holidays, I had to stay on until Christmas because I wasn't 16 until
October. In that time I didn't have any classes at all, I worked in
a zoo on a wednesday and all the rest of the time I ran messeges
for all the teachers and the secretary. Surely it would have been
better if I would have been able to leave and look for a job then
when there was possibly more jobs to look for.

30.    *Male, O grades. Joiner/labourer.*
School was good because it let you go on Day releases to places like
[] – Community centre and other places. My life since I left school
has been very good and I enjoy it to. My School Education didn't
help me at all that much. Since i have left school I have had 1 job
and I have started another. My first job was with Youth
Opperunities Programme. And the job I am no at is with []
MAKING LAMINATED WORKTOPS.

31.    *Female, one O grade. Receptionist for optician.*
I really began to like school from third year on as I got to know my
teacher really well and that really helped me. I did'nt really want
to leave school but all my friends had left and believe it or not that
really made a difference because if you have'nt got a friend you feel
lonely and I did'nt enjoy that much IF my friend had'nt left I would
have stayed on till they threw me out of school.
So just having my friend staying on at school would have made it
better for me.
Since I have left school I have got on fine, I have a steady job and
quite pleased with it.
My school education helped me although I only got the one 'O' level
which would not have helped me in my present job. Before I left
school I really started to come up with very good results in small
tests and my teacher really encouraged me to stay on but as I said
my friend left so I had to leave because I did'nt like being lonely.
My English is the subject I really mean I started to like it much more
than I ever did in my last year at school because this new teacher
came to our school and she really helped me. Also I had a really

good Arithmetic teaher who could'nt believe it when I did'nt pass
my 'O' level Arithmetic.
Well I think that has completed my little sum up of school.
It was a pleasure to help you and hope you understand it and it may
help you a little.
After school hours a school club was held. You could play snooker,
darts, table tennis and badmington at this club. Once everyone had
played around for an hour or two a disco was held.

32. *Female, O grades. Receptionist.*
This may sound silly, but we were *not* taught many "Big-Words" in
English. To hold an adult conversation, one must know some
reasonably explicit words.
I would have liked to have had some debates in English classes for
instance. Maybe Politics or Religion or somthing.
I will be 18 this year, old enough to vote, only I know nothing about
politics. I cannot hold a conversation with my parents or any other
adults on Politics because my knowledge on this is very limited.
Conversation with outsiders is *very* impotant. Many adults my age
go into a job and will not talk to fellow employees, mainly becuase
they do not know how to approach them, how to begin a
conversation.
I must admit I was impressed at my school dance in 5th year. All
the teachers and senior pupils were invited to a small dance hall for
an evening. it was a dinner and disco. The teachers were extremely
sociable. Both pupils and teachers spoke their minds freely, which
led to a most enjoyable evening.

33. *Female, O grades. Housemaid in a hotel.*
Well to start with, due to the state of our country, at the moment,
there doesn't seem much point in trying to help us, youngsters to
study, and to get as many passes as possible. As their chance of
finding employment after school is very bleak. Now a days, the jobs
available which is not many, need no special qualifications as the
most important jobs are all full, as no-one is going to leave, as they
would be thankful they have a job. Also employers no longer have
the jobs to offer or the money to supply any.
But learning does no-one harm, so if they are willing and able, today's youngsters should learn as much as they can. But schools
could help a lot better by pre-paring pupils for going on the dole.
Because the teachers make you thank that you can just walk out of
school and find employment. And if you dont, they consider you

lazy and irresponsible. Personally, I think teachers and carriers officers should spend more time explaining what you do when you have to do when wanting to claim supplementry benifit. As like myself and many of my friends, didnt know where to go and who to see, even the forms were confusing. I just hope that this survey will help school leavers just as much after school, the same as they try when in school, cos once you get in the rut of being on the dole it gets harder and harder to pick yourself up as time goes by, and the months drag by.

34.   *Male, O grades (no A-C awards). Supermarket management trainee.*
I am a trainee departmental Supermarket manager with []. I am in charge of the fresh produce department, which includes ordering and control of Staff, as well as genral dispalying of all the fresh produce. As well as running the department i also traine at all the other department's in the Store. After one year as departmental head i should then be capable of takeing on an undermangers job. At school i really liked classes where the whole class was able to join in and debate the Subject concerned with the teacher. In most of the classes esspecially in 3rd, 4th and 5th year, where you had to sit and copy notes from handouts, or take dictation from the teachers books. My life has changed alot since I left school, I have now got a responsible job, and I am treated more like a mature young adult.
Although i floped when it came to my o levels i still feel that school was and still is a great help to me, in my job, at home, and life. ingenaral. The madger factor in me flopping my 'O' level was the fact that at primary School I was never any good at writing or grammer. I feel that if my teachers there had spent more time on spelling and writeing then I would have probably passed more exams. I feel that in most written exams I knew the answer but because I didn't know how to spell the ansewer I was to embarrast to put it on paper. Spelling will always be my downfall. Please excuse the spelling and writing.

35.   *Male, O grades. Storeman and vandriver.*
My school time was not very good, I did not enjoy school I was made to sit subjects I didn't want to do. Some of the old school rules are needing to be brought up to date.
My life since leaving school has been very successful. The basics

of my education have helped me in my future but the rest is not of much use.

36. *Male, O grades. Unemployed.*
I enjoyed my school education and sometimes wish I was still at school. But it could have been better if I had worked harder in my home and in school.

37. *Male, O grades (no A-C awards). Assistant dairyman.*
Last 6 months was waste of time as I could have started my job, wasn't allowed to leave as I was too young. Most of school hours was wasted doing subjects that was of no help to me in farmwork.
No work experience scheme in farm work (when I was there). I feel that pupils who have a job lined up in the last 6/8 months should be allowed to leave. If they give up this job then they immediately return to school. I was learning more at home with my father than at school, mainly because it was a trade I was taking up.

38. *Male, O grades. Student nurse.*
When I left School in 2nd June 1980 I had already applied for a job as a Student Nurse at [] but at the time I had only 3 'O' Levels But I needed 5 'O' levels so I had to wait until I got my results. I was also too young as you have to 17 1/2. Therefore I was unemployed for 8 months. I was really fed up with this and I suppose I could have done a 6th Year at school but 5th Year was bad enough. The only reason I did a 5th Year was because I needed 2 'O' Levels for the job that I wanted to do but I suppose that's what school is for. Before I went to [] I was away training to be a priest* I don't what it is but the boys there seem to get better marks than average. There were some boys whom I knew who didn't do as well as me in their exams as I did yet because I left and they stayed they got more 'O' levels than I did. I myself think that it was the studeying that they did as they were made to study for 2 hours every night and some of them studied even more than that because there was nothing else to do. Although I didn't do as well in my exams as I would have liked I still enjoyed school at times in fact it was a good laugh at times. In 5th year I went to Paris with the school and that was brilliant.
There are a few things that could be made better e.g. school leaving age could be reduced because there are some people who just aren't interested in school and are just wasting everybody's time including

their. This I think would reduce the classes therefore increasing the time given to each individual by the teacher. I think there should be a time in the day put by for studying, or doing homework. Because while at home there are too many distractions e.g. T.V. Record Players etc. * 1st and 2nd Year at [], and * 3rd Year [] I only did half of 3rd Year here.

39.   *Female, O grades. Sales assistant in department store.*
I attended [] and I think that it is quite a good school. The teachers are very good and they mostly have a good way of teaching you. Some teachers like to leave you to get on with your work on your own, I don't think this is a very good idea as you usually take advantage of it and less work gets done. I have not really settled into a job which I like since I've left school, I feel as though my last year at school was a total waste of time as the O' levels which I received have not put me in the job I would have liked. Instead I am in a job which does not require O' levels or highers. I thought when I was at school that I was doing something worthwhile which would get me somewhere afterwards, but I feel now that it was a total waste of a fifth year. I suppose I could have done better in my Exams and really done well, as what I achieved is definately not enough for what I would like to have been, which was a Secretary. So I think it would be really worth while to devote yourself to a fourth and fifth year at school.

40.   *Female, O grades. Studying at technical college.*
In the middle of vth year I had what is commonly known as a nervous breakdown. I spent a considerable time in a institution whereupon I was unable to do my highers. I felt under the circumstances in which I left I would not make full use of resitting my vth year. As I wished to go into journalism I made enquiries into this with the intention if possible of entry by going to college. I discovered that I was unable without Highers to go either directly or by college course into this field. I was thereupon advised to do a SNC in Business Studies which would on obtaining give me entry to a Communication Studies course which I was assured would count as a qualification in journalism. I latter discovered that I have been misguided and neither Communication Studies or SNC Business Studies would help in the pursuit of my career. I am therefore despite being nearly 18 at the moment trying to enrol at my school [].

I have perhaps not got any further qualifications for the job I wish to pursue, but despite being mis-informed by college tutors etc as to what I should be doing the year has not been a total waste. The year out I feel has equipped me in some ways I feel to cope with the sometimes vigorous demands of Highers. So perhaps by the time this is processed, hopefully I will no longer be classed as a school-leaver.

41.    *Male, O grades. Assistant manager at supermarket.*
I HAVE found that the school was very useful not because of the Educational exams, I have found them not to be relivant but the School helped to condition my mind for thinking (positive). In my opinion if you work hard you will Get on in life no matter if you have qualifications or not. I found my guidance teacher to be very helpful, and the career Service a complete waste of time. Probabley the man than I respected and who had the most impact on my life was a Modern Studies teacher who left our school in the fifth year. [] was his name and I found him to be like a second father to me. He made every body realise if they wanted to be something in there life they had to work for it. By giving examples in his life and who hard he had to work to get where he was.

42.    *Female, O grades. Bank officer.*
From third year onwards the members of staff helped you choose a career that might suit you and discussed all the aspects. The also helped you to choose the subjects which suited you best, If I ever had a problem in eg. English I could always ask my English teacher to explain it again to me and they were always too happy to help. In fact I was quite satisfied with the school I attended. Since I left scool I have understandably lost contact with many of my friends who are still at school. But I seem to have met up with a few again and am able to discuss school with them. Since I have started employment, unfortunately I have not used all the qualifications I have eg. French and History. but Arithmetic especially is a must in a Bank. Also my school education taught me how to meet and talk to new people which is very important again in my line of work. In all I don't think my time at school was wasted at all. It was very enjoyable at the time and has proved useful to me since I began working.

43.    *Male, O grades. About to start on a work experience scheme.*
When I completed this form I was unemployed, but since then I
have just got word that I have been given the chance to start a
scheme, so as I dont know what the scheme will be like, I couldn't
answer the questions.

44.    *Female, O grades. Studying retail design at college.*
The thing that was good about our school was that the teaachers
were very friendly and any of them would help with any problems.
Life since leaving school has been quite good. My school education
has helped me greatly without 'O' levels I could not have entered
my course in College.
Since I left school I was offered a job with the Youth Opportunities
Programme. This job was a Kennel Maid it was really good because
it is something I had always wanted to do. The only drawback was
the pay. I only got 19.50 a week and I had to give my mum 5.00 and
my bus fares were 59p aday which is 2.95. My work started at 8.00
and I didn't finish until 5.00. Which mean't I didn't get home until
5.30 and I had to get the bus at 7.30 in the morning.
I had applied for College but because of a mix up in the post I did
not get accepted because my application arrived too late. Then
three weeks after the course had started a person dropped out and
I was given a place. Since September I have been attending the []
studying to become a retail designer.

45.    *Female, O grades. Studying cookery at college.*
Since leaving [] at 16 years of age I have been attending a course
at [] on Basic Cookery for the Catering Industry which lasts one
year. Ater which I intend to secure work part time and attend
college on day release basis, another year to combine my studies
and experience in the catering industry.
I found the subjects which I choose to study at O' Grade level at
[] most beneficiall to me in the course I am now pursuing. While
attending [] Academy I found the food and nutrition subject very
pleasant because of the modern, well organised and equiped
kitchen and helpful staff. The art department is another area which
has given me a good basic knowledge of design and colour for the
patisserie work I am now doing. The study of Biology has assited
greatly in the first-aid course which I have just finished at the
Technical College.

One subject I was not very good at was Arithmetic and I feel if more tuition were given when one was having difficulties with a particular subject the obstacles could be ironed out.

On leaving school last year I have enjoyed the past months spent at [] enormously. Everything was new to me but I found it an exciting challenge. My fellow students were strangers to me from surrounding schools in the area but all were friendly. Although I have to travel twenty-five miles each way daly I consider this a small discomfort to what I have gained in my training so far.

46.  *Male, O grades. Storeman in textile industry.*
When I was at school I felt like a machine when they put paper and a book in front of you and you were to get it right.
Some of the teachers did try to help. In English the teacher would read a book to us, but we never like the storys and if we told her so she would ignore us. I think the teachers should discuss books which the class would like to read. When I was at school I could not wait to get out and get a job.
But now that I have left school I know I should have stuck into the work I did at school and I would like to back for a second chance.
In my last job, my boss was self employed and did his best to help me to do and understand the job but he was a small firm of only four men including himself working. He had to paiy two of us off because he had no work but he would have take us back on if any work turned up.
The job I have now, in the mills I had to learn by my mistakes becase I was hardly told what to do. But know I am beginning to like it. But if another job better than this comes up. I think I would try for it.

47.  *Female, O grades (no A-C awards). Clerk in travel agency.*
In the school I went to the education was very good, the teachers were nice, plenty variety of things to do eg clubs to join. Since leaving school I feel I have grown up much more and have became independant and can relie on myself.

48.  *Female, O grades. Print room assistant in oil corporation.*
I enjoyed my school life and I believe that my education helped me.
I was put to 'work experience' for one week washing dishes in a

canteen. I hadn't any intention of doing this sort of job when I did leave therefore I think it would be a good idea if some office experience was inroduced – even if the pupil ran errands or just watched the employees of the firm. Even the atmosphere is completely different and the chance of such experience it would help enormously in studies at school. I think that would be of more use to a school leaver than washing dishes would be.

Also, because after deciding that I would leave school, I was changed to a different class (5th year leavers) – unless I had done this, no 'work experience' was given.

49.  *Female, O grades (no A-C awards). Collar linker with knitware mill on day release.*
My school was'nt very strict, that what made it good. My life has been very interesting since leaving school because you are working with people older than yourself and it is different than working with people your own age all the time. My education at school has helped me because we get exams at the technical college.

50.  *Female, O grades. Clerk in builders firm.*
My life at school was fine, but i only wish now that I studied harder than I did. The were plenty subjects to choose from, but in some cases the subjects which you would like to choose were not available. My school education has helped me with my job, but as I never got my English I find it hard to get another job. I am taking my English o grade at nightschool at [] College, which I hope I will pass. I am quite interested in Computers, and hope in the future I will be able to work with them.
When I left school i had all my plant set on going to College, but there again I was not accepted as I never got a pass in my English. I was very fortunate and was able to get a job. I only hope in the future I will be able to find a job that I enjoy doing.

51.  *Female, O grades. Secretarial course at college.*
I am now 16 and an coming to the end of a one year course at [] on Secretarial work. which I have enjoyed doing and I think that that the course has helped me to improve in Typing and learn Shorthand and many of the duties you would have to do in an office.

Before going to College I went to [] and to me it was a good school as the teachers were nice enough and helped with any difficulties we had. I also liked the way the teachers joined in with different activities at the school. It could be made better by the teachers being a bit stricter with some of the pupils. I would also like to see more periods of Physical Education coming in. Since I have left school I have not really had a taste of what it is like to work full time I think I made the right choice in leaving to study for the course I wanted. Also you do not get treated as much like a child at College. I was glad that I tried for as many 'O' levels as the more you have the better I think it is these days. The 'O' levels also helped me to get into my course.

52.  *Male, O grades. Drawer in a textile mill.*
I quite enjoyed my school life, but feel it could be made better with smaller classes, which would result in more individual attention.
I enjoy my job, in which I'm serving a two year apprenticeship. I tried the police force when I left school but I was unsuccessful.
I play drums in a Scottish dance band, and we are making a record soon. We are also going for an audition for BBC Sound Radio.
On the whole my schooling has helped a great deal.

53.  *Female, O grades. Clerk.*
While in my last year at school (4th year) I did not bother to work for my O levels and so did not do well in them. I was supposed to sit 8 O levels but I dropped two subjects, which were Accounting and Geography, and so I ended up only sitting six. Most of my teachers tried to help me in my work but I was just too stubborn and did not listen to them.
When I left school I did not know what my exam results were but did not think I would have done well but I was very lucky in finding a job after being out of school for three weeks (approx.) I left school on the 31st of May 1980 and started working on the 23rd June and have been in the same job since. It is a full-time job which I am very happy in and have no intensions of leaving it as I realise how lucky I was to get it in the first place. I know several people of about the same age as myself who have left school with more qualifications than I have but either did not get a job or have ended up on work experience.

54.   *Female, O grades (no A-C awards). On a YOP scheme.*
      I got on well with my teachers at school they were friendly towards
      me. I quite liked school sometimes. My favourite subject was
      English The teacher really helped me. Since leaving school I have
      been treated like an adult and I have had more freedom. I quite like
      my job as my Supervisor is really nice and there is another six girls
      who I have known for a long time and I get on well with them. I
      have a good nature although I daydream most of the time. If I had
      the chance earlier I think I would have stayed on at school, and
      learned a lot more. The only subject I really hated was P.E. So I
      got changed into ART so I had ART 3 times a week. I think all my
      teachers help me the best they could. and it is true what your
      parents, teachers and other people say school is the best time in
      your life, cause you have time to think what you want to do in the
      future instead of leaving it at the last minute like I done. I have
      enjoyed doing these questions and I hope I have given you all the
      details you need.


55.   *Female, 1 O grade. Apprentice hairdresser.*
      I would just like to say that since I've left school I've been enjoying
      life much better than I did when I was at school. I feel more like
      an adult and I feel more confident with myself.
      School was worthwhile I suppose in some ways afterall you learned
      how to read and write. The last few years of school were a complete
      waste of time for me though I didn't need any qualifications for the
      job I intended to get and I hardly did any work at all thoughout my
      fourth year, as the teachers can't dicipline the pupils enough and
      the classes were too roudy.
      To make the schools better I think the teachers should have a better
      relationship with the pupils because I think they would respect the
      teachers more.
      I have to go to [] for a day release course and it is completely
      different from the schools. The teachers look at you as individuals
      and if you have time for them they have time for you. I feel you are
      treated as an adult and not just a pupil trying to get taught by
      someone supirior.
      There is more freedom in the college and if you pull your weight
      fine, if not its' your life. I think this is what makes you work and
      you also enjoy it this way.
      Any all I can say is I am a much happier and confident person since
      I've left the school. I have no regrets what so ever. Thank you.

56.   *Female, O grades. Studying hairdressing at college.*
The first 3 years at school were very enjoyable and my marks were quite good but I lost interest in 4th year. Teachers were boring in 4th year. Since leaving school life has never been better. My school education has not helped me at all.
At school I lost interest in fourth year when I changed friends, I could have done much better and now regret it.
At college it is up to me to do well because I have chosen a subject that I enjoy and am determined to do well in it, there is all so less pressure at college.

57.   *Male, 1 O grade. Works in coal mine.*
School gave me the chance to sit O levels. I left school after my last O' level and signed on the dole. After not having any luck in getting a job with the carrers I looked for jobs myself. Within two weeks of being on the dole I found a job in [], pushing trolleys, it wasn't much but it was better than being on the dole. I left [] to go to the pit as it was a better job, less hours, better hours and double the money.

58.   *Male, O grade. Works in timber yard.*
I thought that the teacher's of my subjects could have been more cooperative with us. I think that because we were in the bottom course the teachers didn't bother about us. and paid more attention to the higher classes.
the best thing about my school was PE. Because there was plenty to do. Some subjects was so boreing that half of us started to play truent.
I am afraid to say that my education didnt help me one little bit and to be trueful if it wasn't for the law I wouldnt have been at school.
I am quite happy in what I am doing at my work I find it quite enteresting It has lerned me how to measure and handle wood.
ever since leaving school I have lead quite a good life so far. I have met some more new freinds and the money I am been payed is really hellping me alot It's now that I am really finding out how hard it is to become a full time worker it is alot different from School as if to say school was just a waste of time.

59.    *Female, O grades. Hairdresser.*
I left the school and went on to a training scheme in a [] lawyers
office for six months.
I am a bad traveller and didn't want to travel to [] or [] everyday,
that is why I took the job in the hairdressers, There, I am an
apprentice for Three years and go to College once a week for
training.
I have really enjoyed my life after leaving school mainly because
pepole treat you like an adult instead of a child.
My school education helped me because I was offered a job in []
for six months because I had Secretarial Studies.
I think that the schools should do an 'O' Grade in Shorthand.
Because a lot of firms won't take you on without it. If I had had it
I would have been kept on in the job in the solicitors office.


60.    *Female, O grades. Shop assistant.*
School was good in a way as you made new friends, also you had
a best friend but also other very good friends. If anything was
trubling you and you didn't want any relations to know your friend
would always lisen, and help if she could.
Teachers could of controlled the classes alot better.
My school education has helped me a little bit.
Since I left school have enjoyed my Job, Meeting new people,
getting to know other people, helping anyone, also you dont think
oh no school tomorrow. Other people class you as adults when you
dont have to go to school. You dont have to relie on someone else
to buy your clothes, shoes etc. when you are working and bringing
in a wadge.


61.    *Male, O grades. Lab technician.*
I went to [] where I was doing fairly well up until 3rd Year, but 3rd
Year was disastrous I took days of school every 2 weeks and thats
what probably ruined my chances of O' levels. The teachers in []
went out of their way to help me but I didn't listen. If I had the
chance to go back I would jump at it, but as it happens I left. When
I left school I was glad to see the back of the place but soon found
out i was making a big mistake, I soon signed on the dole.
I went to my Careers Office very frequently and I kept filling in
applications for several jobs. I went for an interview, after passing
tests to [] but was told I didn't have enough O' levels to be taken
on. I went back to my Careers Office and finally decided to take

a Y.O.P Course, I did the test and was picked to do a course on Mechanics which was to last 3 months but after 6 weeks I gave it up because having to give my mother money keep me and expenses to and from work I coulndn't keep it up on £23.50 per week as I was getting any expenses it wasnt worth it.

I eventually went for job to [] and got a job as a Lab tech on the building at the [] but I will eventually be paid off in July.

I dont think anything in [] could be made better as the teachers do their best for everyone. Thank you.

62. *Female, O grades. Works in office.*

When I chose my subjects in 3rd year I chose chemistry, but changed it to biology because I never consulted anyone on this I was made to take chemistry. I hated it from the first time I went into the class. I asked repeatedly to be let at into the art class, (I could have taken that as well). They wouldn't let me out and I feel as though I wasted 2 years in a class I detested. I think if you want you should be able to change or use the time as a supervised homework class.

63. *Female, 1 O grade. Unemployed.*

When I left school, I went on the government scheme in the [], I was told after the six months I would be kept on but was not. I left and have been looking for a job ever since.

My school was very bad it was to full of carry-on and if you were in a class beside a lot of trouble-makers to bad you had to stay at their pace of work which was hardly anything at all.

Also half of the teachers were worse than the pupils, they could not control the classes so the pupils did as they liked and some of the teachers would come in tell you to read a page from a book while they would go for a quick cup of coffee.

Since I left school I have been completely bored and fed up with the whole thing. I used to say to myself I cant wait to leave, get a job and work for a living, but now all I do is watch TV and wait for my brew money to come through.

Not all the teachers were as bad as that some of them were really quite nice and helped us alot but that was the minority.

64.  *Female, O grades. Pre-nursing course.*
The college course I was on was a Pre-nursing Course. I wanted to
go into Nursing after I left school and a Pre-nursing course seemed
ideal. I could sit O'Grades and Highers plus gain hospital
experiance. I am sitting 1 Higher and 4 O'Grades. I do enjoy sport
especially fencing and skiing. I do a lot of fencing and train with the
[] Team. Skiing I do for fun and I do not take it as serious as fencing.
After I left school I went to college on the first few days at college
I thought of going back to school but then decided against it, I now
sometimes regret that. At college, one day a week I attended
hospital these were: [] and [] Physco - Gereatric]. I now hope to start
my nursing career at the end of this year in the [].
My school was very good, I felt there was a good relationship
between teachers and pupils. I feel the school could do a bit more
on Careers Information for school leavers, although our school
done a bit more than most. I do feel my school education has helped
a lot. I now wish I had stayed on at school to sit more Highers.
My year at college has been useful that I could sit Highers and
O'Grades plus gain a bit of experiance on the nursing side.
My life has not changed all that dramatically since leaving school.

65.  *Female, O grades. Clerk accountant.*
On the whole I enjoyed school very much. I got on well with my
teachers and my classmates were super. but I really prefer working
I love the job I'm in and the folk I work with are smashing to me.
I don't think I could ever go back to school now. I AM VERY
SORRY FOR THE DELAY IN SENDING THIS FORM BUT I
HAVE JUST RECENTLY MOED IN TO MY OWN FLAT AND
MY FAMILY HAD TROUBLE GETTING THE FORM TO ME.

66.  *Male, O grades. Apprentice turner.*
I am almost 17 years and am 6ft in height. I liked school as I had
good friends and many good teachers. School could be better if in
the last year you were given subjects which were relevant to work,
which you would like to do. my education has helped me. Maths
physics and chemistry. I am taking Engineering drawing at night
school to help me further my career.

67.  *Male, O grades. Apprentice turner.*
     I think that whesn it comes to choose your subjects before you entry
     into 3rd year you should be more details about the jobs in the area
     and qualifications needed.


68.  *Male, O grade. Junior operative.*
     There was nothing good about my school. More sports to do at the
     breaks, If the teachers would pay more attention to you and If all
     the trouble makers were moved out. My life has been great getting
     a job as soon as I did. My school education has helped quite a lot.


69.  *Female, O grades. Unemployed.*
     The only thing I liked about school was, Art, P.E., Arithmetic.
     They had plenty of acivitys at school. Also Good friends. The
     school could be more stricker. Some Teacher are not strik at all.
     They should get more help at school. Since I left school I have felt
     Terrible. No job no money. My school education did'nt help me
     much. I think now that I should have stayed on at school.


70.  *Female, O grades. Studying programming at college.*
     The main thing I didn't like at school was some teachers attitude
     to the pupils after all they must have been pupils themselves at one
     stage. I also don't think you get a wide enough choice of subjects
     it will always end up with you having to take a subject just to make
     up the numbers. Schools, I personally don't think tell you what to
     expect when you have left school and are looking for a job or even
     what to expect once you have got a job. If it could be made possible
     schools should be more like a training colledge preparing you and
     teaching you skills that can be useful when you are in a job instead
     of the things that they teach you now which are hardly any use to
     you when tackling a job. The things I did like at school were the
     people I knew and taking part in sport activates. I didn't realise
     how important not getting my 'o' level English was until I started
     to look for a job. I fell into the trap that most people do that I
     wouldn't write for a job because I didnt like the look of it without
     really knowing what the job was about in the first place. It was my
     mum that promted me to write for the computer course which I am
     now attending and I might add enjoying.

71.   *Female, O grades. Secretarial course at college.*
      I am doing a secretarial course at the [] just now (1 year) it finishes
      at the end of may but if I don't get a job I am going back to do a
      2nd year course
      There was nothing really particular good about our school, Some
      teachers were very helpful (eg typing, English and arithmetic
      mostly) and others didnt atempted to bother just told you to get on
      with your work, but I liked school only for the teachers at our
      school, I think if the teachers nowadays were much harder on you
      and made you work hard, more youngsters would have far more O'
      levels than they've got today,
      My life has been much better since i've left school because now that
      I'm at College I've learned a lot that I've had at school, They treat
      you more like Adults I suppose school has helped us in lots of
      different ways
      In first, second and third year they have a Christmas dance each
      year for them and a go as you please day once a year for the whole
      school and everyone has to pay 10p each and it goes to Charity. by
      the time you reach 3rd year you can go to the Youth Club on a
      Monday night, and in 4th yr and over that (any age) goes on
      Tuesdays & Thursdays. In the school there is all kinds of ativites
      to do eg: MED Dancing, Football, Rugby, Hockey, Basketball,
      Volleyball, Crosscountry running. Debating Society ect ect.
      there is plenty to do after school.
      P.S. The thing I miss about school is my friends

72.   *Female, O grades (no A-C awards). Shop assistant.*
      School was'nt bad on my behalf I think I could have done better in
      my education If I had tried harder. There were others in the class
      who Were Pests who had no Intension of trying and who frequently
      put others off there Work.

73.   *Female, O grades. Library assistant, and studying for Highers at*
      *college.*
      I left school at the end of May, knowing that I had a full-time job.
      I received word a week before I left school that I had the job. I had
      applied to [] College for a full-time Secretarial Course, in case I was
      not successful in getting a job.
      The job was not advertised in the papers, it was offered to school-
      leavers from the surrounding schools. My carears teacher new i was
      intending to leave school after my exams, so she told me of the
      vacancy. (She told everyone else, not just me, but knowone else

from my school was interested.) I phoned and arranged for an interview. There was two jobs going. One in a Branch library and one in the Library Headquarters. Six girls had applied for the jobs and I didn't think I had a chance of getting any of them, but I got the job in Headquarters.

Library Headquarters is not open to the public but the branches are, so, headquarters staff have not only to be trained to do their own individual job, but they have to be trained to do the jobs in the Public libraries, as well, incase someone goes off ill. (which happens quite a lot). I also have to work one saturday in four and I get an extra 3 per cent on my salary for doing so. I never thought I'd end up doing Library work. but I enjoy it quite a lot.

When I started work we had just move into a brand new building in [] This is where all the different departments are gathered in the one building eg. Libraries Dept, Roads Dept, Environmental Health etc.

74.  *Female, O grades. Unemployed.*

I have really nothing to tell you about me, I shall tell you about my school. The thing that was good about school was the teachers some helped you along with your work some werent so nice, on the whole though school kept me and others off the streets because there are no Jobs to get. I don't think that there was anything in school to be made better.

Since I left school, I have tryed to find a job but there has been no luck and I am still trying. I have been on a government training scheme working in [] store I enjoyed doing that but I did not get kept on. The manager said he would have liked to keep me on but because of the current recession he could not. I would not go on an other one. My school education did not really help me at all although it is better to have 'o' Grades than not to have them, it depends on which type of job you are looking for. Sometimes I wish I were back at school but I always ended up losing interest and getting bored. I am bored without a job and I hope I get one soon.

75.  *Male, O grades. Apprentice joiner.*

The belt does not work, lines work better than the belt.

The belt just gives a second of pain While lines you need to stay in all night to do them and so it is a better punishment but even that does not work all the time.

76.   *Female, O grades (no A-C awards). Shop assistant.*
      I have become more self-supporting I buy all my own cloths I give
      my mother money each week. School education did help me but not
      in my O' grades so I attend night school and I am sitting my O'
      grades again. I quite like my job, but I think myself as one of the
      lucky ones at least i have been able to get a job without my
      O'grades.


77.   *Female, O grades. Secretarial course at college.*
      I attended [] and was very satisfied with the attitudes of most
      teachers there, and got on well with most of my 3rd & 4th year
      teachers. I didn't find it too strict or too lenient and mixed well with
      most pupils there. However, I wanted to leave as I did not enjoy
      studying at all and as I intended on doing some kind of secretarial
      work, thought it best to leave at the end of fourth year to attend
      college. If I hadn't received enough qualifications (ie. 4 O' Grade
      passes) I would have gone back for a 5th year. I enjoy college and
      hope my 5 o' Grades will eventually help me get a job along with
      any secretarial qualifications I receive.
      I would like to point out that I think all students attending college
      should receive a grant no matter what their parents earn. There are
      books to be bought and although exam fees are paid back, there are
      still travelling expenses to be paid. I do not live 2 1/2 miles away
      from college but I do travel by bus and none of this money is
      refunded. Only those living 2 1/2 miles from college can get
      travelling expenses.


78.   *Female, O grades. Shop assistant in food market.*
      The school I went to was [] The good things about it was the way
      in which the lessons were taught. Most teachers were eager to help
      you if you were in difficultly but there were always the one or two
      who made you so that you would be frightened to say if you
      understood the subject or not. One of the things I disliked was when
      we had to move between classes because there were so many people
      moving all at once that there were usually great crushes and often
      someone got hurt or pupils were delayed for their classes.
      What could be made better is the organisation of PE classes, late
      changes often made me late for a class. They should have PE before
      lunch or last thing in afternoon so it wouldn't be such a rush all the
      time.

My life has not changed very much since leaving school. At first it was very diferent because my first job was working in a fish factory which I loathed, but it was a job. But during it I kept looking for other and better jobs. It was because of my looking that I saw the advertisement saying that the Food Market I now work in was looking for employees. I am now very happy in my work and have made very close friends who a very pleasent company. The things that happened at school are far and few. I got 2 awards, one in primary school for Scotch Singing, and one in the Academy for PE. I still wonder why I manage to get that because I am not what you would call a fit person. I usually got on quite well with my teachers at school and after I came to like them. Sometime in school when I would be walking along by myself, I would feel that bit frightened because somtimes you would pass a group of pupils who you knew were bullies but daren't do anything about or you would have had it. That is one thing I really disliked about school. That is all I have to say about my school and myself. I hope it has not been too boring to read because I do tend to go on a bit. I hope what I have written will be off some use and will make, I hope, some sense.

79.  *Female, O grades. Works in a bank.*
I am seventeen years of age and left school last year. I was quite glad I left when I did, though I had been planning it from the beginning of the year, when I started writing away for jobs.
The situation of jobs at that time wasn't as bad as what it is now.
I had always wanted to work in a bank and was thrilled when I was offered a job with the []
Since leaving school, I have felt more grown up and I'm treated more like an adult now.
My Schooldays were mostly happy ones. My friends and I joined in a lot of the school Sports. Playing Hockey and Badminton.
My school education helped me so much, but I feel I've learned a lot more since I've left.

80.  *Male, O grades. Electrical engineer.*
When going for a job the applicant can only tell the employer the number of 'O' levels he is sitting and the chances he has of getting them. This is because of the time the intake of apprentaces and the time of the 'O' levels. Most know if they have a job or not *BEFORE* they know there 'O' level results.

81.  *Female, O grades. Secretarial course at college.*
I enjoyed my four years at secondary school. I am now attending further education and I also enjoying it. The course lasts for one year and at the end of it I hope to gain Scotbec certificates. When I leave college I hope to find a job as a shorthand typist.
The school that I attended had a very good range of subjects and plenty of equipment available for the pupils use.
I hope that you find this information sufficient as I have no complaints to make about my school education. I think that my education helped me to gain 'O' Grades and also for me to be able to continue my educaton at college.

82.  *Female, 1 O grade. Studying hotel reception at college.*
Fourth year did not help me in any way. I sat six O'levels all which I passed in my prelims, but I only got one O'level, my english.
I could have done better I suppose, but I was so anxious to leave I couldn't be bothered revising.
I am now just about finnished my course at the college, which is hotel reception and I have enjoyed every minute of it. I am in the proceeds of looking for a job. The only disadvantage of college is that I didn't get a grant, so I won't be able to take another course next year which I would have liked to have done.
I hope I have filled the form in properly and that this information helps you.

83.  *Male, O grades. Deck cadet in Merchant Navy.*
After spending six months as a Deck Cadet, I am convinced that I made the correct decision, and left school just after the start of fifth year. I enjoyed school because the teachers, in general, were young and easy to communicate with, they were also reasonable when it came to discipline. The main problem with my school was the lack of mdern equipment for use in 'practical' subjects. The life upon theocean wave' has been thoroughly enjoyable and as I have stated before I have no regrets about leaving school at the beginning of 5th year. My school education has helped me greatly in my career as I am at present submitting a 'correspondence course' to the Nautical college each month.

84.   *Female, O grades. On a YOP scheme.*
I found that school was good for people with exam potential, but
a waste of time for others. There should be more work experience
for pupils who are not doing an extensive course in exams (eg
Plumbing, mechanics, office work) things which shall help them
when they leave without any worthwhile exam results. Employers
are too choosy about an interviewees dress, I found wearing casual
clothes that I had failed the interview before I had sat down. On
supplementary benefit and living away from my parents I could not
afford to buy an outfit for interviews only as I would not wear one
at any other time. Unemployed PEOPLE ARE PERSECUTED
AND TREATED AS A LOWER FORM IN MANY WALKS OF
LIFE e.g. OLDER GENERATION, TORIES etc. BENEFIT IS
NOT ENOUGH. WHEN I STARTED MY YOP SCHEME I
FOUND I WAS NO BETTER OFF AFTER BUS FARES,
LUNCH MONEY AND OTHER EXPENSES. MY SCHEME IS
FOR PEOPLE WHO MAY HAVE FOUND IT HARDER TO
GET JOBS AFTER HISTORIES OF CHILDREN'S HOMES,
SCHOOL   EXPULSIONS,   SOCIAL   WORK,   POLICE
TROUBLE ETC. I FIND WE ARE TREATED AS IDIOTS
UNABLE TO MAKE UP OUR OWN MINDS ABOUT
THINGS. I HAVE LEARNED NOTHING FROM THE YOP
SCHEME.

85.   *Female, O grades (no A-C awards). Apprentice finisher in printers.*
Since leaving school I can know buy my own clothes and get things
that I couldn't have had before. School has helped me in many
ways. It took quite a while for me to settle down in my job as I was
very quiet and shy, but I have got out of that know and are able to
stand on my own two feet. School also prepared me to move into
work from school, they told me that it would be a big jump.

86.   *Female, O grades. Clerical assistant in insurance office.*
I repeated fourth year in 1980 because I failed 3 of my 'O' Grades.
If I had not done so, I would not be in the position I am now. All
my teachers helped me a great deal in gaining my 3 repeated 'O'
Grades. For me, personaly, Repeating fourth year was very
worthwhile. When I repeated the year I really had a far better
understanding of the courses and could therefore enjoy my school
work far more. In my first 4th Year I was always compeating with
all the other pupils in my classes, without much success, but in my

second 4th year although I had done with work before I could gain
a considerable amount of self confidence within myself and was able
to participate more in class descusions.

I have been working in an Insurance Office now, for 11 months.
Working full time is such a change from being at school. I am now
far more independent, and treated as an adult and have many nice
friends. I really like working in an office, although the work may
be fairly routine, the people at work are all very friendly. Our office
have some really good nights out and have a large party every
Xmas.

I wouldn't say that any particular subject at school has helped me
with my job but overall my school Education and experiences has
helped in a large way to allow me to cope with working life in
general.

One thing that could be improved at school is SEX EDUCATION,
I am fortunative enough in having parents that are prepared to
discuss this topic and to answer any questions at all, but some
parents are very quite about this and rely on Schools to educate
their children. Films should be provided and also regular discusions
should take place.

PS I HOPE THIS CONTRIBUTES SOMETHING TO YOR
WORTHWHILE SURVEY
GOOD LUCK

III  **Highers leavers**

87.  *Male, Highers. Unemployed, and awaiting entry to an FE college.*
The standard of education in the school I went to was good and some of the teacher went out of there road to set up lessons and stayed behind after 4 o'clock to give extra coaching particularly in the weeks before the tests so in that repect I would praise the education system.
However there are several things I would see were with the system as it is now, here are a few examples. Not enough time is spent advising pupils of careers and the qualafictions required and just what sort of things are done in particular jobs. It is understanable that even if these changes were made that some people would end up "on the dole". But here again the system does not point out the alternatives such as College and just what they have to offer.
There are more things which could be done to help teachers such spending more mony on books and improving facalites, but these however can be done gradually with effecting other services ran by the government like the National Health Service.
I fell in to the trap of concentrating to much on getting my 6 "o" grades and 2 Higher's with the result that I am now "on the dole" until I go to the [] in August. Unless the changes that I have suggested are made many more people will end up "on the dole".
*Schools should cooperate more with employer's and find out what they are looking for in people they might employ.*

88.  *Male, Highers. Studying mechanical engineering at university.*
On the whole I think my school life was adiquate, but there is one or two things could be made better. I changed schools in the middle of my secondary education. I moved from [] to []. I feel that my four years at the [] was a waste of time! This is due to the high number of pupils that were only at school because they had too. [] had a very good pupil/teacher ratio with less than 100 pupils. [] only takes students up to O'level then if he/she wants to continue to do highers they have to go to another high school, I went to [] which was 26 miles from my home and I found the difference surprising The attitude was completely different from both pupils and teachers. Because I had been to [] I was at least 6 months be-hind my counter part at [] also at [] I could't do both Physics and Chemistry up to O'level because of this I had to do my Chemistry O Level in 5th year and highers in 6th year which scrubbed out any possibility of SYS.

Like wise I had to do Maths Higher in two years because I was over 6 months behind even though I had got a 'A' in my O'level. I have found lately at University that SYS Maths is very helpful in 1st year. I only wish I had been told (warned) before or during my time at [] of the differences in schools. I feel that [] should either be scrapped or up graded to 6 years On the other hand I give 10 out of 10 for [] as I realy enjoyed my 2 years there.

89.   *Male, Highers. Studying architecture at university.*
In my 3rd and 4th year at school I studied and sat my O levels. The only other activity I took part in except for Clubs out of school hours was Education for leisure. I enjoyed this very much. I 5th year I sat most of my highers and did a few more in 6th year. At the beginning of 6th year I became a prefect a job I later became to detest. My school was very good from the point of sitting exams but did not cater much for the less acedemical and this was a source of much unrest in my prefect days. The head-master was an authoritarian and did not receive much respect from us or his staff due to this attitude. A more easy going person in this position would have been much better.

90.   *Male, Highers. Studying journalism at college.*
School, in not so many words, was depressing. I only remained there up 'till 6th year in order to get enough Higher's to leave School and []. Ever Since I was 14 I have wanted to be a Journalist. Unfortunately before this I picked the wrong course to do so, concentrating mainly on science subjects. Managing to pass these in fourth year, I was *told* that I had to keep up there studies, by certain teachers no matter what my plans. In fifth year I made a complete mess of these exams. If it were not for this I would have been in college by then and would have missed sixth year. However to achieve my ambition I has to stay on, taking up History, which I had always found easy, and gaining the necessary highers. Another thing which annoyed me was the way in which my choice of career was almost totally ignored. Telling the careers teacher I wanted to be a Journalist, I was told that there would be too many applicants and too few places and there was no way I would qualify. Some people would have been put off by this. Two thousand people applied and only 30 were accepted but I was advised to take up Banking or Accountany or something like that. Having got into the college I have enjoyed the best year of my life. I am finally doing

the subjects I want and have enough free time to socialise. If I had paid attention to what I was advised to do at school I would be (a) selling record players (b) working in a bank or (c) a Merchant Sailor. It is time the teacher, and especially the careers advisors listened to the pupils, instead of us listening to them. I was lucky enough to know what I wanted to do but many pupils have no idea and thus end up in a job in which they are bored, tied down and depressed. I hope my answers to these questions can help students in the future with problems such as I have encountered

91.  *Male, Highers. Apprentice technician; day release.*
There are certain parts of this questionaire regarding colleges that I may have missed out or made mistakes in but my position is that at the moment I am full time at [] being paid by my employer and for the next three years will attend this same college 1 day a week.

92.  *Female, Highers. Studying law at university.*
(a) awful that exam results are so dependant upon the ability and eagerness of the appropriate teacher. (b) The lack of opportunity to try what are classed as 'male' subjects (eg technical drawing and mechanics) is prohibitive and in my case may have caused me to waste a year doing a subject at University, doing a subject I do not enjoy (Law) and having to subsequently change after discovering personally what my newly chosen career (architecture) entails - This also illustrates the weakness of careers education, having no real opportunity to discover what you are "letting yourself into" (c) more pupil participation is necessary in school, in order to create a community rather than a 9-400 institution. (d) There should be compulsory and statutory sex Education. (e) Visual aids are more beneficial than merely the written or spoken word. (f) Though economically impractical perhaps class sizes should be smaller. (g) Grading abilities and in this way appropriating classes is a good idea, enabling each to develop at his/her own pace.

93.  *Female, Highers. Studying at university.*
Sixth year was a necessity for 'growing up' since those going on for further education from [] have to leave home. It helped enormously with gaining the right attitude towards study. Academic results weren't, for me, vital therefore school life was more relaxed. The

teachers' attitudes towards 6th year pupils helped us to get used to the atmosphere which is prevalent at university etc; we were treated as adults instead of school children. I enjoyed all my school life and am, at present, enjoying being a student.

94.   *Female, Highers. Shop assistant (bakers).*
School gave me the opportunity to meet and mix with other children. The facilities were good and the standard of teaching was reasonably high, but there were too many pupils. The school was built for 1000, they are already 500 over and planning more, so therefore one loses personal contact with teachers and vice-verse, also with so many children leads to problems with dicipline and being able to control such a number. All in all school helped me though I wish I'd worked harder. As I didn't know what I wanted to do after school, I decided well in advance to take a year off from studying and get my priorities right. I have now been working for a year and earning some money and have been accepted for a course at college so I don't feel that I've wasted my time.

95.   *Female, Highers. Studying at art college.*
School education helped only in providing me with the facilities to study for exams required to enter the course I wished to do. Further education has helped me, the lecturers are interested in my work and not in my appearance (i.e. wearing uniform and having tidy hair etc.)

96.   *Male, Highers. Company director of licensed grocer's shop and garden centre. Day release electrical engineering.*
On leaving school in June 1980, I took up a Summer job as a zoo keeper at [] zoo, until my full time job began in August that year. I began to work on the 4th August 1980 with [], and along with other first year apprentices were sent to the [] for one year's 'off-the-job' training. Here I am taught the fundamental principals of my trade, I also get day release to []. Not only am I taught my trade but are give a fortnights basic training into other fields of engineering, e.g. welding, turning, maching, fitting, instrumentation and sheet metal working.

In my spare time I attend the [] motorcycle training scheme as an instructor, where persons new to motorcycling or people wanting to improve their motorcycling, are taught how to handle their machines and more importantly understand the road and how to drive more safely on it.

School as far as being taught each subject was interesting and enjoyable. The teaching methods in my opinion were very good except when delving deeply into theoretical topics such as Kinetic Theory in physics, and some of the Trigonometrical calculations in mathematics, where I felt the subject became to isolated from reality, having no reference to the practical application of the subject.

My school education has helped me agreat deal, on leaving school (after gaining 'H' grade passes in physics and Engineering Drawing) to take up my full time job, I discovered my two 'H' grade awards enabled me to by-pass the first year of my course at [] and enter straight in the second year.

The only major grumble I had about quite alot of the teachers at [] was the way in which myself and many others from outside the [] town boundry were reguarded as inferior to the town dwelling pupils, in particular to those who lived in the more expensive communities of the school catchment area.

In addition. Higher mathematics I found to be to far removed from it's practical application. i.e. When being taught differentiation and integration, I became quite proficient at both but at the time did not know what its use was. At the end of the one year off-the-job training at [], I was awarded an award for being 3rd apprentice of the year.


97.  *Female, Highers. Studying business organisation at university.*
One reason why I did not enjoy my 6th year at school was because we had far too much discipline imposed on us over trivial matters and possibly not enough when it came to work.

I don't think that there was nearly enough done for us to prepare us for the outside world. All teachers seem to think about is achieving as high standards as possible in as many exams as possible.

I think more should have been done to prepare pupils for University i.e. note-taking. Also, now that I have attended University for two terms, I think that careers advisers make it out to be a far better institution than it actually is. I know I was disillusioned although I still feel that a degree will do me good.

98. *Male, Highers. Studying divinity (theology & philosophy).*
I think it is essential that you know of my past and present educational situation.
I spent my 6 years of "secondary education" in two colleges (the first for only two years and the other for four years). These colleges are different in nature from the "normal" secondary school or college, as they are what are known as *seminaries.* Thus, the environment etc. differ greatly. They were attended by only 130 students on average.
Now, I am attending a "major seminary" in [], Spain.
Therefore, as regards such questions on future career, I am rather "different" – an exception to the norm. Thus, I have found many questions difficult to answer as they have obviously been geared to one who attends school and leaves in search of work or further education.
I hope this makes clearer my situation and throws a little light on my answers. Bye!

99. *Male, Highers. Studying quantity surveying at college.*
One of the particular things about being at college I have noticed is the distance between the student & lecturers. The individual help which is available at college, would help to influence the school teachers & the like. At school I found that the pupil and teacher was much further apart, making it hard to approach teachers on personal problems & other matters.
My school education has helped me in getting to college & that but I think the schools should introduce other things into their timetable other than the usual subjects. For example things like behaviour at interviews, etc. would all help people who are going straight from school into a job.

100. *Male, Highers. Studying at university.*
I have been very lucky to get a place at [] University. I always inteneded to go to college to do a Bed degree at teacher training college. I was told on a college application form I could only apply for one college so I applied to []. My school guidence teacher assured me I would get a place and I never thought about university. However my name was put on the waiting list in the college for some six or seven months. In September when I had left school and was working part time in a supermarket it became obvious I was not going to be accepted. I made 2 later applications

in September 1980 for [] and [] University (two I could go through without UCCA) I was accepted by both and went to []. So I was very lucky to get a place just one month before the start of term and feel angry that the college kept me waiting so long with no word. (I was never given a definite no or yes) I would have had to waste a year if I had not got to University in 1980. Now I'm at University I'm very glad I did not get accepted for college as things have worked out well, but it was close. In 3rd year I only took 6 o grades 2 of which did not offer highers so later on I had a shortage of subjects I could take for higher until others were available in 6th year.

101.    *Male, Highers. Agricultural student.*
[ ] ON THE WHOLE was really quite good. Proper facilities and general lack of money meant we weren't qite as well equipped as some schools in the region. The teachers were mostly keen to see us get on. Although towards the end of my year, many new teachers arrived and the general attitude of discipline, respect etc dropped. Now from friends, gossip etc school life is terrible with many new teachers making the school seem like a play group. If These older teachers had stayed on my final results could well have been better as they pushed you on and you had to do better. Many of my last teachers had a much more relaxed attitude and this meant we slipped back into a easier "working trend". In my opinion many people who werent quite as good as the rest were not helped enough. Maths was my worst subject and although my class and I all tried for "O" grades Maths, the majority never passed. We had a rather poor teacher who gave us all "I d couldn't care less" attitude. If we had, had a better teacher who was prepared to help us fully we would all have tried, that little bit extra to please him. Of course we shouldve done more ourselves but it wasn't that easy.
My life now is very enjoyable, I'm working on a farm, away from home, seeing how other people do jobs familiar to me from experience on my uncles farm. I'm getting a varied outlook in farming in general. I'm to go to [] to further my education in August. If I had gotten my maths I could have sat for my HND which would have given me a better chance in life. Night school or further education would have been rather awkward as I'm well into the hills and away from any real sized town where I could possible have taken more exams. School life helped in a way by discipling me into a working life. I was always punctual and had a perfect attendance throughout my school life so I found it quite

easy to fit into a working week. If I had been lazy and careless during my school days it would have been much harder, changing from school to work. I've never looked back on leaving school in anyway, some friends who have left and have jobs say the same. The only cause for complain is the distance I have to travel home each month to see parents, girlfriend, friends and this, if it could be made better, would make my working life even more enjoyable than it is. On the whole I'm happy with my education past and hopefully to come from college, my job is interesting and enjoyable, so I am very lucky to be in the position I'm in now.

102.  *Female, Highers. Studying English at university.*
      The school which I went to I did not like at all. The work, particularly in my last two years, was rushed and I felt that we were trying to cram too much in, in too short a time. Also, I may be being unfair here, but the general impression I got was that most of the teachers did not care at all about the pupils, and very few were able to control a class without use of a belt, which is ineffectual (at our school anyway) or sarcasm which led to antagonism.
      The difference between school and university was far greater than I had anticipated as a result I find myself struggling to cope with the work. I dont think sixth year helped at all, the tutors at [] are far more helpful than any of my teachers ever were. The prospect of finding a job after leaving university is something I try not to think about at the moment – but being at university is the most enjoyable part of my education so far.

103.  *Male, Highers. Studying quantity surveying at college.*
      I felt that sixth year was a waste of time as we were given no freedom + treated like first years.

104.  *Male, Highers. Studying business administration at university.*
      SCHOOL EDUCATION LACKS IN ONE MAJOR AREA. ITS SCOPE OF TEACHING METHODS ARE TOO LIMITED AND SPECIFIED AND SO FAIL TO PREPARE A CHILD FOR THE WIDE SPECTRUM OF DEMANDS SOCIETY WILL MAKE OF HIM WHEN HE LEAVES SCHOOL. SUCH A DEFIENCY IS PARTICULARLY HARMFULL WHEN

THE PARENTS OF THE CHILD CANNOT PROVIDE HE
OR SHE WITH A *BALANCED* EDUCATION.
MULTIPLICATION AND CHAUCER'S POEMS ARE NOT
EVERYTHING IN LIFE

105. *Female, Highers. Studying primary education at college.*
I really enjoyed school, but I feel that in fifth and sixth years there
should be more preparation for pupils like myself who go on to
continue their education at college or university: in regard to such
things as (it may seem very simple) writing your own notes which
you have not had to consider at school where we more or less
depended on the teachers for producing notes etc. Another aspect
of fifth year is that of the hugh jump in work and demands from
'O' grade to higher subjects. I personally feel that there should be
an intermediate level and highers should be sat in sixth year,
because as it stands I feel that a sixth year is a wasted year for the
pupil who has acquired all his entrance requirements for further
education and I myself decided to leave school after fifth year
when I passed my highers and was accepted for teacher training
college because I felt that if I went back to school for a sixth year
I would be wasting the teachers' and my time studying for SYS
exams which I wasn't wholeheartedly interested in!

106. *Male, Highers. Assistant gardener.*
The school I attended, [], in [] on the hole was quite good but far
too large, aprox. 1800 students, as a result the close relationship
between pupil and teacher did not occurr untill well into fourth
year. This relationship is of the upmost importance for the
progress of the pupil.
The size of the school again played a great part in the use of career
guidance which appears to be absent from this form, just like in
school. The most advantageous time for a pupil to start thinking
about a career and to be guided towards any thoughts is halfway
through fourth year.
The point of guidance in careers is very important and largely
underated in many schools.
I, personaly, have experienced this *"Guidance"* in fith year I had
actually chosen in my mind the main subject/or carrer which
interested me and wanted then to be guided as to which subjects
to consentrate on and what courses were open to me in University
or College. The proper guidance was not given to me by the

*"trained"* guidance staff but the job left to our head of upper school who did his best to guide me although he did not know a lot about my chosen carrer (HORTICULTURE) or even how to obtain the information. There must be other students who faced a simillar dilema as my own. Because of this lack of guidance I made some important mistakes in subject choice and concentration which resulted in my not getting to University to study a BSc in Horticulture.

I have now, through other souces i.e. friends and aquaintances, obtained acceptance to a Horticultural college in [] and I am at the moment working a years experience work. A lot of time and education was wasted in my case because of this lack of *proper* guidance in careers.

107.  *Male, Highers. Studying biology at college.*
I entered an HND BIOLOGY COURSE AT []. I have now left this course and I will be starting a new course in late August. I decided to leave the biology course because I was completely disillusioned by the course and the attitude of the lecturers. When I decided to leave the course, and had been accepted to the other course, I went to my senior lecturer and told him my intentions. About a month later when I was handing in my library books and locker key, he asked me why I was not filling in a questionaire about second year. I told him that I was leaving the course and he was surprised. This gave me the impression that he was not taking a great interest in his students – You believe that you will be treated like an adult at college. I was'nt, the lecturers tended to look down on myself and my fellow students. As a result I lost my interest in Biology and science subjects and I am now taking a course in communication studies which I hope I will enjoy.

108.  *Male, Highers. Studying science and technology at college.*
In Total I spent 6 year at school – repeating First year. In the 6 years I spent in school life I must say that on the whole it was a worth while experience.

In my first year at secondary school I was placed in a remedial class. This experience had a great influence on my future work throughout secondary school. It showed me that in order to get anywhere in society today qualification are necessary. After being giving the chance to leave the remedial section I found I had a natural liking for Chemistry biology etc little of which had been taught to the remedial classes

The teaching in the remedial classes was on the whole more personal in which a greater teacher – pupil relationship was built up due perhaps to the smaller classes. The rest of my school life up to 5 year lacked this personal touch with the class being to big.

The subjects I disliked in school were basically the art subjects such as English History and geograph. Modern Studies however I found interesting since it taught you something of polictics and society today which is alway useful

The science subjects were to me always more interesting Physics however was always out of reach due to my lack of knowledge of maths. I had been asked to drop this subject at the end of 2nd year. This I think is one of the great faults in my school education during 5th year I realised this and attempted to sit o' grade maths in one year although I did not get it, I am attempting it again this year. The reason for droping maths can again be traced back to my time in the remedial classes where mostly only arithmetic was taught.

At present I am in first year at []. The classes which are totally science are smaller than that in school and the atmosphere is generally better. I think this is due to being with other people not all of the same age group who are interested in studying the same thing.

The lab work at college is also much better throughout secondary school lab work had almost always been done by the teacher but at college you have to learn to be able to cope for your self. This is one thing school life did not teach.


109.    *Male, Highers. Studying maths at university.*
        In general, school education did not prepare me well for life after school, but there is not much more it could have done for me. Obviously, my school education has helped me as I am now at University but the subjects given at school & the way they are taught, differ a great deal. for example, school classrooms are smaller & have less people than University lecture theatres & the practice of taking notes from a lecture is quite difficult to begin with. On the whole, although school education is limited, there is not much more it can do.

110.    *Male, Highers. Audio assistant trainee in broadcasting.*
        MY *MAIN* REASON FOR LEAVING AND NOT GOING TO
        COLLEGE ETC. WAS THAT I WAS FED UP WITH
        THEORETICAL WORK BUT WANTED PRACTICAL
        WORK.
        THE SIXTH YEAR STUDIES CERTIFICATE I SAT IN 6TH
        YEAR WAS DONE WITHOUT ANY "OFFICIAL" CLASS
        TIME, IN SO MUCH AS I WAS GIVEN BOOKS, A
        SYLLABUS, NOTES, SOME LAB FACILITIES AND A
        LITTLE HELP FROM AN EX-SCHOOLTEACHER (2 HRS A
        WEEK) TO DO MY STUDIES.
        TO EXPLAIN, MY SCHOOL DIDN'T HAVE THE STAFF,
        EQUIPMENT NOR CLASS TIME TO OFFER ANYONE
        DOING A SIXTH YEAR STUDIES COURSE. THE OPTIONS
        BEING (1) DO IT YOURSELF OR (2) GO TO THE
        NEIGHBOURING SCHOOL, [], TO STUDY THE SUBJECTS
        WANTED. THE LATTER WAS REJECTED AS THE UPSET
        OF MOVING FOR 1 YEAR WOULD'VE PROBABLY
        AFFECTED MY OTHER STUDIES.
        I DID NOT MOVE TO ENGLAND IN SEARCH OF A JOB,
        AS IT MAY SEEM, BUT WAS SENT THERE AS PART OF
        MY TRAINING FOR MY JOB IN []. I APPLIED FOR THE
        JOB IN 1979 AND SPENT MY 6TH YEAR REALLY
        WAITING FOR MY 18TH BIRTHDAY SO THAT I COULD
        JOIN THE [].
        LIFE SINCE THEN HAS BEEN BLISS!!


111.    *Male, Highers. Studying applied physics at university.*
        THE WHOLE SCHOOL SYSTEM IS WRONG, PEAPLE IN
        SCHOOLS ARE TAUGHT NOT TO BECOME
        INTELLIGENT AND USEFULL HUMAN BEINGS BUT
        ARE PROGRAMMED TO PASS EXAMS. WHILE THIS
        MAY LOOK VERY NICE ON PAPER IT IS NO GUIDE TO
        THE PERSONS INTELLIGENCE. IN SCHOOL CHILDREN
        ARE TAUGHT NOT TO HAVE INQUISITIVE MINDS AND
        BECOME INTERESTED IN EDUCATION BUT RATHER
        FORCED INTO CERTAIN CLICHED SUBJECTS AND
        TOLD TO PASS EXAMS.
        THIS ASIDE, THE FORM I FOUND PARTICULARLY
        SEXIST E.G. IN THE LAST PAGE A GREAT NUMBER OF
        QUESTIONS ARE ASKED ABOUT THE FATHERS
        OCCUPATION WHILST ONLY ONE QUESTION IS ASKED
        ABOUT THE MOTHES OCCUPATION . I'M SURE MY

MOTHER WOULD BE VERY OFFENDED IF SHE SAW HERSELF BEING GIVEN SUCH A DEROGATORY POSITION. THIS ONLY SERVES TO CONTINUE THE AGE-OLD MYTH OF THE FATHER BEING THE BREAD WINNER. AND WHAT OF ONE-PARENT FAMILIES WITH ONLY THE MOTHER WORKING?
ALSO A NUMBER OF THE QUESTIONS I FOUND THAT TO JUST ANSWER YES OR NO WAS NOT ENOUGH THEY REQUIRED MORE COMLEX ANSWERS E.G. ON PAGE 3, QUESTION 1 IT ASKS IF MY PARENTS WANTED ME TO STAY ON FOR ANOTHER YEAR, WELL IN MY CASE MY PARENTS LEFT THE DECISION UP TO MYSELF BUT THIS CONTINGENCY IS NOT CATERED FOR IN THE QUESTION.

112. *Female, Highers. Studying secretarial course with languages at college.*
I was never given much advice, if any on what I could do when I left school. I knew I wanted to do something with my languages and typing but the reason I went back to school for a Sixth Year, apart from being a bit young to go to University or College was the fact that I had no idea of what I wanted to do and I could not discuss it with any one at school.
Obviously my school education has helped as without it I would not be at college as I needed 1+ highers and o levels to get in. My school was selective and it went comprehensive this year before I started. The teachers were set in their ways, and it sometimes appeared to me that the teachers were of the opinion that because we were the "Comprehensive" years we were not as "bright" as the selective years which I objected to very much.

113. *Male, one Higher. Football player.*
I HAVE A PART-TIME JOB. I AM A PART-TIME PROFESSIONAL FOOTBALL PLAYER WITH [] FOOTBALL CLUB. I TRAIN 2 NIGHTS PER WEAK AND PLAY FOOTBALL ON SATURDAYS + SUNDAYS AND SOMETIMES DURING THE WEEK. I HAVE BEEN DOING THIS FOR 2 YEARS SINCE I WAS SIXTEEN YEARS OLD. I STAYED ON AT SCHOOL SO I COULD SIT MY HIGHERS WITH A CHANCE THAT I COULD GET THE JOB I WANTED WHEN I LEFT AT THE END OF FIFTH YEAR.

BUT SO FAR I HAVE NOT BEEN ABLE TO FIND WORK.
DURING MY FIFTH YEAR AT SCHOOL I WAS TRAINING
2 NIGHTS PER WEEK FOR [] AND TODAY I AM FULL-
TIME WITH THE CLUB BUT I AM STILL LOOKING FOR
JOB AS I WOULD RATHER HAVE A FULL-TIME JOB
AND PLAY PART-TIME FOOTBALL.
I ENJOYED MY SCHOOL-LIFE AT [] AND WAS QUITE
HAPPY THERE FOR MY FIVE YEARS. THE TEACHERS
WERE VERY FRIENDLY AND IN LATER YEARS I
BECAME VERY GOOD FRIENDS WITH MOST OF THEM.
I COPED WELL WITH THE WORK AND COULD
PROBABLY HAVE DONE BETTER IF I WAS'NT SO
INTERESTED IN MY FOOTBALL CAREER. THE
ACTIVITIES AT SCHOOL WERE GOOD. I PLAYED
FOOTBALL FOR THE SCHOOL FOR FIVE YEARS AND
PLAYED FOR THE TABLE-TENNIS TEAM FOR TWO
YEARS AND THERE WAS PLENTY OF OTHER
ACTIVITIES THROUGHOUT THE SCHOOL. I ENJOYED
MAKING MORE FRIENDS AND MIXING WITH PEOPLE
FROM OTHER SCHOOLS AND BECOMING MORE
CLOSER TO THEM DURING THE FIVE YEARS SPENT AT
[] SECONDARY. MY LIFE SINCE LEAVING SCHOOL HAS
BEED QUITE EXCITING. MY FOOTBALL CAREER HAS
BEEN THE CENTRE OF EVERYTHING I HAVE DONE. I
HAVE WORKED MY' WAY UP TO EVENTUALLY
PLAYING FOR THE FIRST TEAM WHICH IN ITSELF WAS
A GREAT EXPERIENCE AND HAVE LEARNED A LOT
ABOUT THE GAME IN THE LAST TWO YEARS. I HAVE
ALSO BEEN QUITE DISAPPOINTED IN NOT FINDING A
FULL-TIME JOB BUT I AM STILL KEEN TO FIND ONE AS
STAYING ON FOR MY HIGHERS WAS THE MAIN
REASON FOR DOING A FIFTH YEAR. SINCE LEAVING
LAST YEAR I HAVE HAD QUITE A FEW INTERVIEWS
FOR CLERICAL JOBS BUT HAVE BEEN UNSUCCESSFUL
WITH MY APPLICATIONS EITHER BECAUSE I AM OVER
QUALIFIED OR MAYBE ITS BECAUSE I AM TO OLD (MY
OPINION)
MY SCHOOL EDUCATION SO FAR HAS NOT HELPED IN
THE SENSE THAT IT WOULD GET ME A JOB BUT IT HAS
HELPED ME IN OTHER IMPORTANT WAYS. EXAMPLES
OF THIS ARE THAT I CAN COPE WITH THE OUTSIDE
WORLD TO A CERTAIN EXTENT BETTER THAN
OTHERS, AND HAVE QUALIFICATIONS TO HELP ME
FIND A JOB WHICH I WORKED HARD FOR DURING MY
SCHOOL CAREER. ALSO IT HAS HELPED ME

PHYSICALLY AND MENTALLY AND HAS GIVEN ME GREATER KNOWLEDGE IN THE SUBJECTS I STUDIED AND AT THE END HOPEFULLY A MORE MATURE PERSON.

114.  *Female, Highers. Studying mathematical sciences at university.*
I enjoyed school but I was also taught that you had to work. Unfortunately at school we did not have a language lab like many other schools and we also had no computer although I now believe the school has one. I am enjoying University but am finding the work hard and unfortunately you are not pushed to work like at school. I am glad that I stayed at school for highers as I feel that school was not a waste of time and I managed to achieve something.

115.  *Female, Highers. Studying chemistry at university.*
There should be regular "check-ups" on the standard of teaching of the staff of the school as this has a very important part to play in how a pupil does in his examinations. There should also be specific teaching courses which lecturers at universities should have to attend as at the present after having obtained a certain standard of degree anyone can lecture.

116.  *Female, Highers. Studying maths at university.*
I am at present at [] doing a BSC degree in Maths. At school in 6th year, I took 2 Math CSYS papers (I &II) thinking this would help me understand better the course I would be taught at University. Paper II is comprised of (a) Calculus and (b) Analytic Geometry and Vector.
We never were actually *taught* Paper II at all. In our maths period, we were given a room to sit in and given a bundle of notes (rough notes) and the appropriate Calculus book. We were not given the appropriate Geometry and vectors book until approx 1 month before exam. And were given no explanatory notes to this, just the breif summary in the book, if we were completely stumped, there was a teacher we could go to, while he was teaching another class. He would help us with Calculus and come from the Geometry side. We were taught no vectors, and so going into the exam we were certain that this would mean we would be unable to tackle 2 of

the question. (We were supposed to be given a choice in the exam, because we could not answers 2 of the questions we had no choice) We had 2 teached for Paper I, these teachers split the teaching between them and this was well taught.

The reason for all this was the shortage of maths teachers in our school. As we were going into 6th year the maths teacher who had taken us through from 3rd year, who was an excellent teacher, had just left. This left us for Calculus a teacher we weren't very sure of and because he mainly always was with other classes due to the Math teacher shortage in the school it was awkward to always keep interrupting his lesson.

O levels and highers are generally well taught at [] but while I was there, (it may have changed now I found the were not capable of providing adequate CSYS coverage possibly for most subjects, definitely for maths due to shortage of teachers. However, the knowledge we did gain in CSYS Paper 1 has helped with the coure I am at present doing. More generally I find school education helpful, - little education is useless. I am of the opinion that if one possesses O' levels and Highers that on the whole Employer will choose these people for jobs as opposed to unqualified applicants. The fact they have O levels and highers shows they can take a task seriously and look at problems in an organised manner instead of panicking and backing away from them.


117.   *Male, Highers. Studying quantity surveying at college.*
       In second year the guidance to which subjects taken was terrible.
       Now up in [] doing a course which I dont like, seriously thinking of chucking, it ie poor guidance.
       In class the same people always got picked on, to many teachers favourates. Disrimination which is unfair. The hours of school are too long, like colleges there should be given a half day once a week.


118.   *Female, Highers. Auxiliary nurse.*
       My School education has played an extremely important part in my life so far. Although your capapabilities may reach University level, it is your personality which dominates your success.
       In my opinion my school couldn't have done any more to help me because by the time you reach your teens very little can sway your diligence with your studies, indeed it might only succeed in encouraging contempt.

119.   *Female, Highers. Studying for SCOTBEC secretarial certificate.*
When I first attended [] it was only a 4th year school. When our
parents heard of this a steering committee was formed to have the
school up-graded. My Father served on this committee and is Past
President of the Parent-Teachers Association which was formed
after the success of the Steering Committee. I found that my 5
years of secondary school life have been quite pleasant and that
most of my teachers were very helpful regarding my school work.
I had seriously considered remaining at school for a 6th year, but
after the H grade exams of 1980, I was advised by the Deputy
Rector to leave and go to college, as the subjects which I would
have liked to have studied were not available due to lack of
teachers, money and accommodation.
however, I have now decided that when I leave college in June I
will take up an offer in the Unites States of America, as I feel that
my career prospects in Scotland are extremely bleak.

120.   *Female, Highers. Studying business administration at university.*
I liked school but now like the freedom of university. Higher
economics and accounts have helped me as I am doing these
subjects at university.
The school I went to was over 400 years old and therefore had very
established ways to do things. It turned comprehensive recently
and is having slight problems with the new pupils. It is having to
change in order to deal with the non academic pupils and new
subjects are being made.
I am glad I am out of the school as the standards are deteriorating
and is not now the school it used to be.

121.   *Female, Highers. Studying geography at university.*
While at school I took part in many activities Country Dancing,
badminton, school shows and choirs and the Duke of Edinburgh's
Award Scheme in which I did many varied activities such as
community service, hiking and camping, first aid, squash.
All this made my time at school very enjoyable. As well as these
activities I went on several residential trips with the school. These
and the after school activities helped me to get to know my fellow
pupils and teachers better. My school offered a varied selection of
activities especially for one week in June known as 'Choice
Activities Week'. We had the choice of doing things such as
cooking, golf, hill walking, day trips, and trips abroad and in
Britain for the week.

Since leaving school I have not taken part in any such activity but am going to try and join some sort of club. I feel that part of learning should also include these activities which give us the chance to meet people and become more interesting people I think it is a very important part of school life and should be stressed move while at school so that we will continue it out of school.

122.    *Female, Highers. Doing secretarial studies at college.*
I feel relationships between myself and my teachers were quite good and I could talk to them quite easily about my school work but I feel relationships between heads of departments and pupils could be improved. I also feel the careers service at the school should be better eg. you are treated O.K. if what you want to do is the same as the majority ie college or going into an ordinary job but if like myself you wish to do something different eg. theatre work, stage dancing. you are convinced that it is an overcrowded profession and you haven't a chance of getting in.
Since leaving school I have been studying for an HND (SEC ST) at [] in []. I am not enjoying the course, not because its hard work but because I know it's not for me. I know I will stay on until the end of this 1st year but after that depends on exam results.

123.    *Female, Highers. Clerical assistant with the DHSS.*
I enjoyed being at school because it was a small country school and you knew everybody. The teachers knew us all individually. I enjoy life much more now that I have left school as I really enjoy my work and think that it has helped me to grow up more. My school education hasnt realy helped me at all I have learned more since I left school. I also admit I didn't study at school because I hated studying and always left it to the last minute before exams.

124.    *Female, Highers. Studying veterinary medicine at university.*
I found that my school was helpful in directing us towards careers. In 4th and 5th year we received many lectures on various types of employment, college courses, universities etc.
Our school, in my opinion, gave a high standard of education which obviously helped me to get the necessary qualifications for university entrance.
I felt that 2nd year at school was a waste of time because the classes were not streamed and there were too many people who had no

intention of sitting 'O' grades in the same classes as those who were trying to get on well. As a result much time was wasted which could have been used to push on those who intended taking 'O' grades.

I think 'O' grades could be missed out by pupils who show enough aptitude for higher grade work. In my school we started work for Higher Maths in 4th year before Christmas and had to stop about March and go back to 'O' grade to do some revision. We were not given the choice of missing out the 'O' grade stage which I think should be made available to all pupils.

I think pupils should ry to aim for some career early in their secondary education especially if qualifications need to be of a high standard. Knowing that you need say 5 highers at certain grades certainly makes you work harder and makes you determined to succeed.

My school education enabled me to get into a course at Uni which I enjoy very much though there has been some difficulty in bridging the gap between school and University. I think that the reason why this happens is because of the type of lessons we get at school. They should encourage us to write our own notes etc and try and make school-teaching in 5th and 6th year more like Uni lectures etc.

After the initial settling down stage at Uni, I seem to be coping well enough – and I do think that my school education prepared me reasonably well for university.

125.  *Male, Highers. Construction worker.*

For me, school in fifth and sixth year, was just a waste of time due mainly to myself. O-Levels were obtained easy enough with out doing too much work and I thought highers would be just as easy. By attending class you would practically be given them thats what I went thro' 5th year thinking. Boy, was I wrong. Two years wasted!

What could be made better? When I was at school I felt I was just another student. Nobody cared if I was working, doing homework, as long as I attended that was all they were worried about. So to better it I think there should be more teachers with upto date equipment, ie books, smaller classes.

Also, I think the whole timetable should be looked in to, with less emphasis on subjects like Latin, History, Geography, and more on Physics, Chemistry Maths & Modern Studies. And also a better balance of theory & Practice. and people to help school leavers cope with the world, after leaving school.

In these days of high unemployment, one cannot be too choosy, if at all, about the job he/she is offered. As in my case. This was the first job I had a chance at so I took it to start with hoping I would get a better job some where else. A year has passed now and still nothing. So I'm stuck with a job now with no trade or qualifications at the end of the day and no chance of getting a trade now. I'll probably go thro' life now an semi-skilled man with a semi-skilled wage and live happily ever after. Also another thing if there are any apprentiships or trainees going they are being filled in by the Job Creation people where the employer get six months free labour, and after that if there no good He can just let them go.
THANKS MAGGIE THATCHER?

126.  *Female, Highers. Clerical assistant for government body.*
In my opinion [] was an excellent school to attend as the teachers took an interest in most of the pupils and if someone had a problem, not only in school work, maybe a personnal problem they were only too willing to solve IT. The teachers also helped to guide you into taking the courses in which they thought that you would be successful in.
I feel that some subjects do not prepare you for leaving school and getting a job. The subject which I feel was useless in preparing me for the job that I am in was Secretarial Studies. In this course you were told certain ways to set down a letter and of how office Procedure would run. But WHEN I entered my job I learned that things run quite differently in an office from what YOU ARE taught at school.
Now that I have left school I must say that I am releived that I have at last got a job but i must state that I throughly enjoyed the school. Sometimes when I am at my work I miss not being at the school and I wish that I were back attending it. I miss some of my friends who have stayed on for a sixth year because along with the teachers we used to have some good fun.
In my view third, fourth and fifth year all stand out in my mind as being the best years that I have ever had at school because that is when the teachers began to treat you like an adult and you got a bit more responsibility.
It is only now when I am out working that I realise and fully aggree with the saying, "School days are the best days of your life"

127.   *Female, Highers. Bank clerk.*
       I am basically a very quiet person although not someone who could
       be called shy. I did not mind school although I cannot say that I
       enjoyed it all the time. There were times when I would have loved
       to pack up. Studying often got me down. There were times when
       you felt lonely if your group of friends were in a different class.
       at school I think you rely on awful lot on friends. If you have good
       friends whom you can relax with life is much happier. I enjoyed
       fifth year and sixth year at school, mainly because all my best
       friends stayed on as well, and others whom we were not friendly
       with left school. In fifth year relations with teachers greatly
       improved. Sixth year was quite good as we had our own common
       room (although the year tended to be split into several groups, not
       all on good terms). The teachers & head teachers however had
       really little knowledge of the pupils. This was seen in the choice
       of prefects. Not those popular with the other pupils, but those who
       were very confident and chatted to all the teachers. Often they
       were popular with the teachers but disliked by all other pupils
       apart from their own group of friends. I feel that sixth year helped
       prepare me for work. I felt too young to start work at the end of
       fifth year.
       Although looking back, no matter how you are treated in sixth
       year, even when the teachers talk to you as adults, I felt that I was
       still at school and this made me feel young. School, no matter how
       much I sometimes disliked it was a safe place to be. It was a secure
       place, rules had to be obeyed but if broken – punishments would
       be given. We could be late for class – (and often were) In sixth
       year, we often skipped certain periods. This is not being
       responsible but we knew it was school – not for real as it were.
       I feel I have grown up very much since leaving school and
       beginning work. I feel however my school should have tried to
       prepare us for work a little more than it did.


128.   *Female, Highers. Studying science at university.*
       My school was small compared to others (about 800) so, at least
       in fifth and six year, nearly everyone knew each other so no one
       could be too lonely. Some of the subjects were taught quite well
       with good teachers on the whole (one or two very poor
       exceptions). The language department was very poor.
       Careers at school was practically nil – no properly trained teachers
       who sometimes gave the wrong information which occasionally
       ruined people's plans for the future.

Only 1st and 2nd year Catholics got proper RE. 3rd and 4th year were given modern studies by a lapsed Catholic who I don't think knew what religion to teach us.

Not many organisations in school life (partly due to lack of interest from pupils).

129.    *Female, Highers. Studying ecological science at university.*
What I feel most strongly about after leaving school, was the amount of guidance I got there. As you can see from the form I did the 3 O-grade Sciences but in different years at school. No-one even mentioned the fact that O-grade Chemistry (or even Higher) would go well with O-grade Biology. This is not to discredit the teachers who had too big classes, too much work ad did not even know you very well at the end of second year when the critical choice was made. I frankly did not know what I wanted to do, so I was no help to them either. Of course alot people did make the right choice but that was probably because they (or their parents) knew exactly what they wanted to do and how to go about doing it. I also received 2 careers interviews which I found no help at all, although this was my fault as I still did not know what I wanted to do. The career's officer did susgest university so maybe they were some help. I just wanted to voice my general dislike to the way subjects and careers are picked.

130.    *Female, Highers. Apprentice dental technician.*
I would never say that the years I spent at school were a waste of time. If anything school helped to develope my outlook on life. Although I must admit that I had not planned to leave school when I did, (at the end of 5th) I think mainly I was scared because I did not know what to expect. But I would not blame this on the teachers, as no matter what you are told about jobs etc it is only natural that you are scared to leave school, where are dependent on others, no matter how independent you think you are, you are always relying on friends and teachers.

I enjoyed school, I think basically because I was popular, had many friends and acquaintances, and enjoyed being with the teachers and learning (occasionally).

I regret having not studied more for my Highers. At the time I was in "the couldn't care less stage". I don't know if I could blame anyone but myself. But I do feel that at this time, between prelims and exams, pupils in 5th year should have been made to study or do more written work although the actual course had ended. Maybe the pupil should strive to study at this time, but everything is so relaxed at school between prelims and exams that everything is dropped, including study which I'd imagine this time was designed for. I couldn't really blame the system, I would say that it was my laziness to blame.

I am however very lucky to have landed a great job, earning the exact wages of any male in the same profession (which is rare). I was also lucky to get the job as it is basically a male dominated field - DENTAL TECHNOLOGY.

It is interesting and I am able to use my artitstic skills to their full. I am also sitting my appreticeship at the best possible place as the Dental Hospitals calls for very high standards. I would I was one of the lucky ones!

131. *Female, Highers. Studying for a degree in outdoor education.*
Since leaving school I have embarked upon an career in outdoor education, at []. The school I previously attended, [], gave me a good foundation for the course I am now doing, but this was only because it was done outside the school timetable. I feel that more outdoor education should be made within the reach of all pupils, especially seniors as they are often not permitted to attend specialised courses which could benefit them in this area.

132. *Female, Highers. Studying O grades at college.*
After leaving school I went to college against the advice of my guidance teacher. I now regret having made that decision as I will be giving up my course of study in June 1981 instead of completing my two year course. This will please my mother immensely because she is always talking about my lack of money. I have applied for nursing (general) and hope to be accepted.

133. *Male, Highers. Studying physical education.*
I enjoyed my school life very much. This enjoyment was brought about by friends, teachers and my parents. Sport played a very important part in school and so in my life. As I enjoy nearly every sport this aided my enjoyment of school. School also gave me many opportunities to try out many different activities eg scouting, pipeband, CCF, and many others. Since leaving school I have engaged in a P.E. course, have attemped to become an RAF Pilot

without success but will try again and hopefully succeed. I have moved home with my parents to the south of England, this has brought new opportunities and many new friends. I work part-time in a disco in [] and part-time for [] in the Motorcycle division. These are just holiday jobs until college resumes in September. I have found that everything I learnt at school has been useful to me at sometime or in someway since leaving school.

134.    *Female, Highers. Shop assistant (temporary).*
Since leaving school I consider myself to be very fortunate to have kept in employment. I have decided on a career in business and have applied to [] for management trainee. I did not get in and have now applied to [] and [] and I am awaiting results. If I do not get in to either of them I have an unconditional place at [] to do business studies.
At school we totally lacked a careers service that was of any use. Staff were willing but there was an ignorance and as a result the pupils did not benefit from their assistance. I think school should have a practical as well as academic side in preparation for working life, interviews etc It would also be helpful to have careers guidance to give you an idea of the sheer variety of jobs available
On the positive side I feel that school was great fun and I thoroughly enjoyed my years there. But it is only once you have left you realise how sheltered an environment it was. I think it comes as quite a shock when you leave as you have a total sense of freedom and you are not exactly sure what to do with it.
I have found in interviews the personnel officers are amazed that school leaves have little idea of interview procedure and no idea at all of how to "sell" themselves. In these days of high unemployment it would surely be a good idea for schools to help their pupils in this way.

135.    *Female, Highers. Studying hotel catering and institutional management.*
What I felt was good about my school was the fact that the teachers made it obvious that they were generally interested in you and your future. Although we did not have a careers mistress, which is a point that I do feel requires some attention, each individual teacher was willing to discuss career prospects with his or her subject.

136.   *Male, Highers. Unemployed.*
Since I left school in June 1980 I have been unemployed. For this
I blame the current recession and myself. Myself, because of the
lack of thought I gave to my career while at school especially in
the first and second year. I regret this due to the lack of "scope"
my qualifications give me for seeking jobs (no science, or technical
subjects). College or night school may be a method of gaining
more qualifications but as now i am still undecided and generally
confused. Just a word about Sixth year. I repeated my fith year in
the hope of getting O grade Maths which I considered important
and also to give me time to mature and think about what was to
come after. Looking back now and taking into consideration my
present situation it did not do me all that much good although I
did pass Maths (really another higher is needed due to standards
needed today). However having a sister who is interested in
university etc. Sixth year is excellent for preparing a person for
further education like this.

137.   *Female, Highers. Doing Scottish studies at university.*
After writing so much about what I'm actually doing I feel I ought
to stress that I didn't make a conscious decision about going to
University. I drifted in and immediately became disillusioned by
its scruffiness and impersonality. It compared very badly with the
well-equipped and relatively small high school which I attended
for five years.
I came to University because I didn't feel confident about getting
a job. I was afraid of being stuck in a boring office job surrounded
by middle-aged people. University has helped me in many ways.
It has broadened my experience, given me more self-confidence.
Unforunately it has also shown me that I was never cut out for the
academic life. At school I had teachers who encouraged me,
praised me when I did well and in the hope of more praise
motivated me to do better. That aspect is completely missing from
University and I find I have no motivation to succeed whatsoever.
My final year at school was not a particularly happy one. I was
anxious to leave, anxious for the freedom which university seemed
to offer. I played truant quite a lot but such was the atmosphere
of the school that so long as my work did not seem to be suffering
my teachers, or at least some of them, were prepared to accept it.
The same behaviour at Uniersity is apparently ignored. Until, that
is, you find out youve been disqualified from sitting the end of
session exams. This arises, no doubt, from the belief that at
seventeen or eighteen a student should have a measure of
responsibility for his or herself.

If I could leave University immediately I would do so. However I have an obligation to my parents to at least try to succeed. Giving up anything in these days of recession is looked on with disgust, but I would rather be on the dole doing at least some of the things i wanted to do than stuck in a college or university doing almost nothing and feeling guilty about it.

I always thought I was lucky in going to as good as school as []. When I was there I thought of it more in terms of academic success but since leaving I realise now that some part of its success came from a sense of community, a belief that at least some of the teachers cared a little about you.

If I were in a position to influence Scottish education policy I would say that far more important than subject cirricula and fancy school equipment is having schools small enought to care about their pupils.

138.    *Male, Highers. Studying electronic engineering at university.*
I don't feel there was anything outstanding about my school, but I would have liked to see more mature treatment and responsibility given to 5th year pupils after all one could have left school by then and have started a family.

I feel that the belt should *not* be used at all after third year at school, since it would be absolutely degrading for any near-adult to be treated in this way.

Since leaving school and entering university I have enjoyed life much more. There is a greater amount of independence and one learns to rely only on their own ability. It is for this reason that I would like to see full grants for every student, regardless of parental income.

It's a stupid question to ask whether my school education has helped me – its obvious that I wouldn't be where I am today without it, and nobody would not be affected, for better or worse, by it.

At school I consider myself to have been rather shy, and nothing at school changed this until later on, and this change was not due to the school.

Finally I appreciate how this survey may help future school pupils but why wait until a year after I have left shool to ask me about my fourth year – 3 years ago. There is much that I have forgotten, which could have been of more value if found out at that time.

139.    *Female, Highers. Studying English at university.*
        I sat GCE "O" levels in England then my family moved to [] where
        I sat SCE Highers. I found that there was not much difference in
        the standard of work between "O" level and Higher, except in
        French where the jump in the work was noticeable. The jump
        between the standard of French required to pass the Higher and
        the standard of French at University was so great I could not catch
        up on the work and I have had to drop French.


140.    *Female, Highers. Doing diploma in primary education.*
        I really enjoyed school and I did not want to leave. Every-one
        wanted me to leave after fifth year and go to college but as I was
        too young to apply for teacher training and as I failed two highers,
        I ended up doing a sixth year. My sixth year was my best year ever.
        We were a really small sixth year and we all go to know the
        teachers very well. (Most of them knew me already).
        My main disappointment in school was my performance in SCE
        higher exams. I had managed to get through O grades without any
        studying at all and I tried to do the same with the highers. The first
        time I only managed two Highers but I got the other two the
        second time. I would have liked better grades but I think I got
        more than I deserved.
        At school, in my first and second years I was in every activity
        except the electronics club It all became a little hectic and from
        third year onwards I just concentrated on hockey and a bit of
        badminton. I attended every house games night and I really got
        a lot out of school. It just proved what the teachers' always told
        us in first year that we would only get out of the school what we
        put into it. In my final two years I was on the house committee.
        I was the house Vice-Captain twice, although in fifth year the
        actual house captain was never at school. She was a 6th year and
        they never had very many classes so we rarely saw them. Therefore
        I was left in charge quite a lot. In my own 6th year it was a lot
        easier. I had more time to sit back and watch the house captain
        get on with it.
        When I left school and went to college I felt really lost. Every-one
        in first year had to live in residence. No-one else I knew was doing
        the same course as me so I was completely on my own. There were
        others just like me and I soon met a whole new set of friends. I'm
        more often down in [] now than I am at home. I feel as if I've
        matured greatly since leaving school. I think that last year at this
        time I was sitting behind a desk at school with a teacher telling me
        what to do. Just now I'm on teaching practice at a primary school

and I don't even look old enoght to have left school myself. It really amazes me what the college has done to me. I was never really shy but I would never have done half of the things I'm doing now when I was at school.

As for living away from home, its great. We have so much freedom. I even got in a bit of studying for my last exams and I find I'm becoming quite studious. At the weekends we can do more or less what we like as long as we don't disturb other residents.

I still keep in touch with some of the teachers from school. They are still as nice as ever and very helpful. The college staff are the same – nothing's a bother to them.

I hope I've not written too much of my life story to bore you. There is so much more I could tell you but it would go on and on. I've always had the gift of the gab. I hope what I've told you is helpful however. I've probably answered the question all wrong as usual but here's hoping.

141.    *Female, Highers. Clerical assistant.*
What I liked about school was that most of the teachers were quite young and they could join in the fun that you were having. Also because they were young, they could understand the problems that faced teenagers more than older ones because they had just finished their teens. Also the teachers helped to give us a lot of activities outside school hours which showed that they were interested in us because they were not getting paid for doing this.

What I didn't like about school is that when I was a prefect in fifth year, I found that most of the teachers didn't respect us for what we were doing. In times of crisis, you would hear the teachers saying let the prefects do it, its not our job, when it was their job to look after the pupils in their school. Also you didn't get a bit of thanks for it, they say if you want to wear the prefect badge then you've got to work for it.

I believe that my school education helped me to get my job because the school taught me how to sell myself at an interview. I also believe it will help me for a future job because I want to commit myself to the police-force and they said that if I received my higher English then I would be considered, therefore it could help me there.

Another thing about school that was good was that we had very good and of the highest quality teachers, if it wasn't for their interest in me and good teaching I don't believe I would have passed my exams.

May I point out that if I were to choose a school to go to, I would pick my old school [] because although they made you work hard they realised that you also had to have a little play too.

# Index to Part II. A Cross-Section of Comments

The index numbers refer not to pages but to the numbering of the quotations in Part II.

# Appendix 1. Representativeness

How representative are the young people whose comments appear in Part II? A detailed account of the 1981 survey is given by Peter Burnhill in Appendix 1 of *Fourteen to Eighteen*. It concludes:

> [I]t is estimated that 96 per cent of the nominal target population were on the sampling frame, of whom 88 per cent agreed to co-operate in the survey; 84 per cent of the nominal target sample were therefore sent a questionnaire. The rate of contact was high (fewer than 5 per cent were eventually [returned to us as] "undelivered"), as was the response rate to the questionnaire (at almost 90 per cent). The achieved sample therefore succeeded in covering about 72 per cent of the nominal target sample. (pp.235-236)

Despite the very high response to the questionnaire (about 90 per cent) and the reasonably high coverage of the target sample (about 72 per cent), there were detectable biases in the usable sample that the survey produced. The net effect was that leavers with Highers qualifications were over-represented and those with no formal academic qualifications were under-represented.

The main point at which this bias arose was when the sampling frame was constructed. This happened when the young people were still at school. They were each asked for some personal details, such as their home address, and also whether they wished to co-operate some nine months later with the proposed survey. At that stage pupils who were eventually to leave school with no academic qualifications declined to co-operate in larger proportions than did pupils who were to leave holding examination certificates. Of those who did agree to receive a questionnaire, a higher proportion of non-certificate leavers could not eventually be contacted at their home address than was the case among their counterparts who left school with academic qualifications. Thus some bias in sample coverage occurred before the young people received the questionnaire.

Among those who received the questionnaire, there was little variation in response rates between leavers with different levels of qualifications. Among those who returned the questionnaires, young women were more likely to accept the invitation to comment (40 per cent) than were young men (31 per cent). Respondents who had attempted only O grades were less likely to comment (29 per cent) than were those who had attempted Highers (43 per cent) or those who had attempted no SCE examinations (34 per cent). The table compares the 141 respondents whose comments constitute Part II with the population of school leavers in 1979/80. The over-representation of those achieving Highers passes and the under-representation of those with no academic certificates is apparent. Details of qualifications and of sex are given for each respondent in Part II, and the reader may wish to make a rule-of-thumb adjustment in forming an overall impression from the 141 comments as a whole.

### Highest level of SCE qualification

|  | in the population of school leavers 1979/80* | in Part II |
|---|---|---|
| Higher passes | 28 | 39 |
| O grade awards | 42 | 41 |
| none | 30 | 20 |
| total % | 100 | 100 |
| total number | 89928 | 141 |

*leavers from special schools are excluded

There was little indication that respondents had more often been moved to comment by bad experiences, or *vice versa*. In a separate question all respondents were asked whether their last year at school had been worthwhile. The probability of a written comment was not associated with a "yes" or a "no" answer to this question. Nor were the young people more or less likely to comment by virtue of what they were doing at the time they answered the questionnaire, be they in a job, on a government scheme, unemployed, or in a full-time course. (The one exception was non-certificate women leavers on government schemes, fewer of whom offered comments than did other non-certificate women leavers.)

The respondents whose comments are included in Part II are therefore broadly representative of all respondents to the questionnaire, when representativeness is judged in terms of a measure of general attitude to school, or of career in the nine months after school. But respondents were themselves not fully representative of the population of leavers, and this is one reason for the discrepancy shown in the table. One source of bias was the more frequent "contracting-out" of eventual non-certificate leavers, and the bias was compounded by the problem of making postal contact with them. It cannot be said for certain whether or not young people who are difficult to contact through the post, or who decline to co-operate in a survey before they receive the questionnaire, are a representative group in other respects. But it is likely that they are not and that included among them are higher proportions of the alienated, disaffected or inadequate young than are to be found in the general population of young people. If so, the comments in Part II present a more sanguine picture of the situation at the time of the survey than that which actually obtained. In analysing the data numerically in *Fourteen to Eighteen* it was possible to make adjustments for such biases. To repeat, the reader may wish to bear in mind the under-representation of non-certificate leavers in Part II when making any overall judgement, and also to recall that the respondents whose comments figure in Part I were selected not for their representativeness, but for the intrinsic interest of what they had to say.

A.F.McP.

# Appendix 2. Questions

Different questions or back-page prompts were used in different questionnaire versions. Below are listed all the prompts which appeared on different questionnaire versions for the 1981 survey, divided according to whether the questionnaire was sent to non-certificate leavers (questionnaires A and B), leavers with O grades (questionnaire C), or leavers with Highers (questionnaire D).

## Non-certificate questionnaires (A and B)

Version: 1.    **(Further education)**
Would you like to tell us more about yourself? What was good about your school? What could be made better? Has your school education helped you since you left school? Did it encourage you to try for college? If you are in a job, has your employer encouraged you to go to college? If so, how have you got on? Please tell us about the things that happened at your school and after.

2.    **(S3/4 O grades and choice)**
Would you like to tell us more about yourself? What was good about your school? What could be made better? Has your school education helped you since you left school? Did you get the chance to study for the O grades (or O levels) you wanted in 3rd year and 4th year? If not, why was this? Did you have to do prelims? Did you want to sit the O grade exam? What were non-certificate classes like? Please tell us about the things that happened at your school.

3.  **(Life since leaving school)**

    Would you like to tell us more about yourself? What was good about your school? What could be made better? What has your life been like since leaving school? Has your school education helped you? Please tell us about the things that happened at school and after.

4.  **(Last year at school: value of courses)**

    Would you like to tell us more about yourself? What was good about your school? What could be made better? Has your school education helped you since you left school? What do you think about the courses you studied in your last year at school? Were they interesting? Useful? Did you like the way they were taught? Please tell us about the things that happened at your school.

5.  **(Guidance and careers)**

    Would you like to tell us more about yourself? What was good about your school? What could be made better? Has your school education helped you since you left school? Did you see your guidance teachers at school? Did you want help from them? Did they help you? Were other teachers helpful? And the careers officer? Please tell us about the things that happened at your school.

6.  **(Last year at school: Christmas leavers)**

    Would you like to tell us more about yourself? What was good about your school? What could be made better? Has your school education helped you since you left school? What do you think about the courses you studied in your last year? Did you leave school at Christmas? What was school like for Christmas leavers? Please tell us about the things that happened at your school.

7.  **(Jobs and YOP)**

    Would you like to tell us more about yourself? What was good about your school? What could be made better? Has your school education helped you since you left school? What things have you found difficult when looking for a job? What do you think should be done to help young people who are looking for jobs? What do you think of the government's special schemes for unemployed young people? Do they help young people to find jobs? Do they help them in other ways?

8. **(The perfect school)**
Can you tell us what your perfect school would be like? What would you do there? What would the teachers be like? Would you have to go? Would there be any rules? And how would your ideal school compare with the school you actually went to?

## O grades questionnaire (C)

Version: 1. **(Further education/Higher education)**
Would you like to tell us more about yourself? What was good about your school? What could be made better? Has your school education helped you since you left school? Did it encourage you to try for university and college? If you are in a job, has your employer encouraged you to go to college? If so, how have you got on? What have you found too difficult or too easy? What has been disappointing? What have you enjoyed? Please tell us about the things that happened at your school and after.

2. **(S3/4 O grades and choice)**
Would you like to tell us more about yourself? What was good about your school? What could be made better? Has your school education helped you since you left school? Did you get the chance to study for the O grades you wanted in 3rd year and 4th year? Could you take the subjects you wanted in the O grade exam? Please tell us how your subjects were decided and about the things that happened at your school.

3. **(Life since leaving school)**
Would you like to tell us more about yourself? What was good about your school? What could be made better? What has your life been like since leaving school? Has your school education helped you? Please tell us about the things that happened at your school and after.

4. **(Value/interest of O grades)**
Would you like to tell us more about yourself? What was good about your school? What could be made better? Has your school education helped you since you left school?

What do you think about the courses you studied for O
grade? Were they interesting? Useful? Did you like the
way they were taught? Was the amount of time you had to
spend on work for exams about right? Please tell us about
the things that happened at your school.

5. **(Guidance and careers)**
Would you like to tell us more about yourself? What was
good about your school? What could be made better? Has
your school education helped you since you left school?
Did you see your guidance teachers at school? Did you
want help from them? Did they help you? Were other
teachers helpful? And the careers officer? Please tell us
about the things that happened at your school and after.

6. **(Last year courses: Christmas leavers)**
Would you like to tell us more about yourself? What was
good about your school? What could be made better? Has
your school education helped you since you left school?
What do you think about the courses you studied in your
last year? Did you leave school at Christmas? What was
school like for Christmas leavers? Please tell us about the
things that happened at your school.

7. **(Jobs and YOP)**
Would you like to tell us more about yourself? What was
good about your school? What could be made better? Has
your school education helped you since you left school?
What things have you found difficult when looking for a
job? What do you think should be done to help young
people who are looking for jobs? What do you think of the
government's special schemes for unemployed young
people? Do they help young people to find jobs? Do they
help them in other ways?

8. **(The perfect school)**
Can you tell us what your perfect school would be like?
What would you do there? What would the teachers be
like? Would you have to go? Would there be any rules?
And how would your ideal school compare with the school
you actually went to?

## Highers questionnaire (D)

Version: 1.  **(Further education/Higher education)**
Would you like to tell us about yourself? What was good about your school? What could be made better? Has your school education helped you since you left school? Did it encourage you to try for university and college? Or if you are in a job has your employer encouraged you to go to college? If so, how have you got on? What have you found too difficult or too easy? What has been disappointing? What have you enjoyed? Please tell us about the things that happened at your school and after.

2.  **(S3/4 O grades and choice)**
Would you like to tell us more about yourself? What was good about your school? What could be made better? Has your school education helped you since you left school? Did you get the chance to study for the O grades you wanted in 3rd year and 4th year? Could you take the subjects you wanted in the O grade exam? Please tell us how your subjects were decided and about the things that happened at your school.

3.  **(Life since leaving school)**
Would you like to tell us more about yourself? What was good about your school? What could be made better? What has your life been like since leaving school? Has your school education helped you? Please tell us about the things that happened at school and after.

4.  **(Value/interest of O grades)**
Would you like to tell us more about yourself? What was good about your school? What could be made better? Has your school education helped you since you left school? What do you think about the courses you studied for O grade? Were they interesting? Useful? Did you like the way they were taught? Was the amount of time you had to spend on work for exams about right? Please tell us about the things that happened at your school.

5.  **(Guidance and careers)**
Would you like to tell us more about yourself? What was good about your school? What could be made better? Has your school education helped you since you left school?

Did you see your guidance teachers at school? Did you want help from them? Did they help you? Were other teachers helpful? And the careers officer? Please tell us about the things that happened at your school and after.

6.  **(S5 Highers: courses and exams)**
    Would you like to tell us more about yourself? What was good about your school? What could be made better? Has your school education helped you since you left school? What do you think about the courses you studied for Highers in fifth year? Were they interesting? Useful? Did you like the way they were taught? Was the amount of time you had to spend on work for exams about right? Please tell us about the things that happened at your school.

7.  **(Jobs and YOP)**
    Would you like to tell us more about yourself? What was good about your school? What could be made better? Has your school education helped you since you left school? What things have you found difficult when looking for a job? What do you think should be done to help young people who are looking for jobs? What do you think of the government's special schemes for unemployed young people? Do they help young people to find jobs? Do they help them in other ways?

8.  **(The perfect school)**
    Can you tell us what your perfect school would be like? What would you do there? What would the teachers be like? Would you have to go? Would there be any rules? And how would your ideal school compare with the school you actually went to?